DAMON
Beyond The Glory

By Damon Bailey

With Wendell Trogdon

Damon Bailey
P.O. Box 1143
Bedford, Indiana

Backroads Press
P.O. Box 651
Mooresville, IN 46158

ISBN 0-9724033-2-9

Printed by
Country Pines, Inc.
Shoals, Indiana

CONTENTS

LIFE IS GOOD

It has been almost a decade since Damon Bailey was an all-American at Indiana University, four years longer since he led Bedford-North Lawrence to the 1990 state high school championship.

The roar of the crowd now sounds for others. The limelight has dimmed. Sports writers seldom call for interviews. His legendary basketball career is now documented in history and stored in the minds of his fans.

But for Damon Bailey, life still is good.

His thrills come not from swishing jump shots from behind the 3-point arc, soaring for dunks or making crisp passes for assists. His contentment comes as a husband, father of three, a successful businessman and a casual fan.

In a sequel to *Damon - Living A Dream*, he reviews his role as an unassuming Hoosier icon and details his transition to life away from the media spotlight.

And he reveals his thoughts about the enigma of Bob Knight, his coach at Indiana University, high school basketball under Indiana's one-class systems, and about fatherhood, business, politics and dozens of other topics. In *Damon - Beyond the Glory*, he gives readers for the first time thoughtful and intriguing views on incidents and events that have shaped his career.

BACKGROUND

Date of birth: 10-21-1971. Parents: Wendell and Beverly Bailey, Heltonville, Indiana. Attended Heltonville Elementary School, Shawswick Junior High and Bedford North Lawrence High School, a 1974 consolidation of Bedford, Heltonville, Shawswick, Tunnelton, Oolitic, Needmore and Fayetteville. Graduate of Indiana University in 1994.

Married to Stacey Ikerd August 12, 1995. Three children: daughters Alexa and Loren, son Brayton. Residence: Rural Lawrence County, not far from the high school he and Stacey attended.

An owner of Hawkins Bailey Warehouse in Bedford. Also involved in other ventures.

Height: Six feet three. Playing weight 200 pounds.

SETTING THE STAGE

THE STAGE: Notre Dame University. The championship of the national AAU basketball tournament for players 11 and under has been decided.

The Indiana team has won the game and the most valuable player is Damon Bailey. The choice is so obvious no vote needed to be taken. He will reveal later, "It was a special moment for me. I realized for the first time that I might really accomplish something with this game called basketball."

It was a prelude to championships to come.

* * *

The STAGE: Shawswick gym, where elementary students from Bailey's hometown of Heltonville, attend junior high. Crowds pack the bleachers for each game to see the talented eighth grader. Coach Bob Knight joins them to watch and is impressed. "He is better right now than any guard we have (at Indiana)," he tells a writer who uses the quote in *Sports Illustrated*.

Expectations of greatness may be a burden to others. They will not be for Damon Bailey. Within a year his Bedford North Lawrence team will make the first of three Final Four appearances in the Indiana state tournament.

* * *

THE STAGE: Scottsburg High School gym, November 22, 1986: Bedford-North Lawrence opens the season with an

82-70 victory over Scottsburg. Freshman Damon Bailey starts, scores 20 points, hits 10 of 12 free throws, and has four rebounds and two assists.

THE STAGE: Barney Scott gymnasium, Seymour, March 10, 1990: Bailey takes a lob pass from teammate Chad Mills, eludes two Scottsburg defenders and scores. The basket gives him 3,020 points for his high school career, one more than the mark set in 1961 by Lewisville's Marion Pierce. It is a record yet to be broken.

THE STAGE: The Hoosier Dome (now called the RCA Dome) in Indianapolis, March 24, 1990. A record crowd of 41,046 fans, including 500 reporters and photographers, watches the drama on the floor between Concord and the Stars of Bedford North Lawrence.

No one notes the hour on their watches. Time is forgotten, except for the figures on the scoreboard. That clock shows 2:38, as in 2 minutes 38 seconds to play.

Coach Dan Bush calls a time out. "Get the ball to Damon," he tells the team. Damon is Damon Bailey, a senior who set the state career scoring record two weeks earlier against Scottsburg.

Bailey soon hits two free throws. At 1:45 he scores on a drive, is fouled, hits two free throws. The Stars have cut the deficit to 58-57. Bailey grabs a rebound of a teammate's shot and scores on the put-back. His team takes the lead, 59-58.

Concord scores and BNL trails, 60-59. Again the Stars go to Bailey. He is fouled, hits both shots, and BNL leads 61-60. The clock reads :38, but it will seem an eternity before the game will end.

A Concord player misses a free throw and Bailey is fouled. He steps to the line. The pre-dawn hours he has spent back shooting at the gym in Heltonville pay off. He hits both shots. Bedford North Lawrence wins, 63-60.

Bailey's team is the state champion and he is named winner of the Trester Award for sportsmanship and leadership. His name is written forever into the archives of Indiana high school basketball.

*   *   *

Marian's Home Cooking, a popular dinner in Oolitic two miles from Bedford, opens as usual, expecting its usual lunch time crowd. No one — not a single customer — shows up. The would-be diners are all in Indianapolis or glued to their televi sion sets watching Damon Bailey, coach and Oolitic native Dan Bush and the BNL Stars play at the Hoosier Dome.

It will be the first time the diner goes without a lunch crowd in 13 years, recalls owner Bob Pettyjohn.

THE STAGE: Assembly Hall, Indiana University, a Saturday afternoon in early March.

Damon Bailey has played his final home game as a Hoosier, a career that earned him a spot on I.U.'s All-Century team. The speaker, as seniors are honored, is coach Bob Knight, the Hoosier mentor who will be fired in 2000.

"For four years, I've probably been Bailey's greatest critic, but I also think for four years I have been his greatest fan.

"I don't think there's anybody in this building who, as an 18-year-old or a 40-year-old, has been in quite the position Damon Bailey was when he came to Indiana. Was he a combination of Jack Armstrong, Superman, King Kong, Magic Johnson, Larry Bird? Was he a little of all these things or was he an 18-year-old kid who wanted to come to Indiana and play basketball, and play for a coach who wanted him to be all those things, I guess, all the time?

"Maybe nobody who ever played in the Big Ten was in first place as much as Damon Bailey (referring to the team's 108-25 record and one NCAA Final Four appearance from

1990 to 1994). In that span the Hoosiers went to each NCAA tournament winning an I.U. record 11 NCAA Tournament victories."

Knight mentions the game that had just ended, a 78-65 victory over Wisconsin in which Damon scores 19 points and had eight rebounds, eight assists and three steals. It was Indiana's 44th straight home victory over the last four years. The coach continues:

"He got a tip-in, he posted, he shot from the outside, he drove, he made a half-dozen great passes for baskets. I saw him guard a guy twice . . ." said Knight, the needler, sprinkling his remarks with sarcasm.

He added, "He played today when most of us probably wouldn't be able to walk. We don't make a big thing out of injuries, but this kid — not just here, but I can go back to each of the other three years, when I simply said, 'Are you going to be able to play?' And he said 'Yep!' A hell of a lot of players would have said, 'Coach, I can't.'

"Never did he say that."

Knight asked, "Was Damon a guard? A forward? A center? Maybe he was a little bit of all those people (Superman, Jack Armstrong, Magic Johnson, King Kong) I mentioned. Maybe he was a little bit of guard, and a little bit of forward and a little bit of center. Maybe there really wasn't a position to put him in out here.

"What he was, was one hell of a basketball player," Knight concluded.

THE STAGE: Various Indiana gymnasiums, the spring of 2003. Damon is leading the three Indiana University senior players on a barnstorming tour across the state.

It has been four years since he played and he has seldom touched a basketball in the interim. Yet he scores in the 20s in a number of the games, hitting for 37 against a team in Plymouth. Thirty of those points come on 10 three-point shots.

CAREER MILESTONES

Lest Damon in his modesty forget to cite his achievements we list them here in abbreviated form, for there are many.

* Most valuable player in 1983 on his national championship AAU team of players 11 and under.

* Led his teams to three Final Fours in the Indiana high school basketball tournament four years.

* Was named to *The Indianapolis News* and Associated Press all-state first team four straight years.

* Propelled his team through tenacity to the 1990 state high school championship.

* Won the prized Trester mental attitude award at the state finals that year.

* Ended high school career with 3,134 points, a record that still stands, averaging 28.4 points per game. He also had 551 assists (6.9 per game) and 969 rebounds (8.8 per game). Helps his team, coached by Dan Bush, to a four-year 99-11 record.

* Was named Indiana Mr. Basketball and helped lead his Indiana team to two wins over a rival Kentucky all-star team.

* Was inducted into the Gatorade Circle of Champions as the national high school player of the year.

* Received the Naismith Award.

* Named the high school player of the 1981-1990 decade.

* Was Big Ten freshman of the year, third team Big Ten as a sophomore, a Big Ten honorable mention as a junior and was named to the all-Big Ten first team as a senior.

* Named third team All-American as a senior.

* Finished his I. U. career with 1,741 points, which leaves him in 2003 in the seventh spot. At the time he graduated he was first in the number of 3-point shots scored, tied for second in assists and was seventh in free throws. He played on teams with an overall record of 108-25 and appeared in the 1992 Final Four. Bailey played in an IU-record 11 NCAA Tournament victories.

* Later was among 15 former players chosen for the I.U. all-century team. It was an illustrious group that included Steve Alford, Walt Bellamy, Kent Benson, Quinn Buckner, Calbert Cheaney, Archie Dees, A.J. Guyton, Alan Henderson, Bob Leonard, Scott May, George McGinnis, Jimmy Rayl, Don Schlundt and Isiah Thomas. The fact the 15 were chosen from a group of 38 former all-American players at Indiana made the selection even more special.

* Drafted 44th in the 1994 National Basketball Association draft by the Indiana Pacers.

* Won all-conference honors as a member of the Fort Wayne Fury of the Continental Basketball Association and was named player of the week.

* Was among CBA players chosen to represent the USA in the Pan-Am games in Winnipeg, Canada, in 1999.

AS OTHERS SAW HIM

By WENDELL TROGDON

On the surface, it appears Damon Bailey now lives in a world far removed from basketball. He's a businessman, a husband, father of three, still as unpretentious as he was when a teen-age idol.

Few indications of his hardwood career are in his office at the Hawkins Bailey Warehouse in Bedford. An emblem of an Indiana University jersey with his Number 22 is interwoven in the carpet. No trophies are on display, just two basketballs with no indications of their significance.

He works not in an ivory tower or atop a high rise office building. The warehouse is in an old Reliance Shirt Factory, his office in the sub-level, just across a wall from the heavy-duty maintenance products his firm sells. Its location is like that of high school coaches of another era, down a hall, off the basketball court.

Pretension is as absent as it has been throughout his fabled career.

The phone rings not for interviews, but for business. His thoughts are not on the next game, but on the challenges of his competitors. His conversations are interrupted to answer questions from his sales force or offer them advice. He treats them as equals.

At least once each week, he takes to the road to contact customers in an area that stretches from beyond Louisville into Illinois and over much of Indiana. The business is as much about service as it is supply and distribution and his travel may result in 12-hour days.

He is no different than most men. He and wife, Stacey, spend most of their free time with their three children. They attend games at Bedford North Lawrence High School, he to watch the action on the floor, she to observe the cheerleaders she coaches.

He is at Indiana University for some team practices and most home basketball games, watches road games on a big TV screen at home.

Each summer he conducts basketball camps across the state for pre-teens, teaching them the game and helping them learn life's values. It is a payback, he says, for all that the game and the fans have been for him.

He looks fit enough to play four years after he gave up the rigors of professional basketball. And he still does at times, joining graduating I.U. seniors and former teammates in a series of barnstorming games in the spring of 2003.

He still needs no last name for identity. Mention Damon and most Hoosiers assume the name goes with Bailey. Only Oscar as in Robertson is as recognizable. Even icons like Larry Bird and Steve Alford need their last names as identifiers. So does the governor.

No other Hoosier — not Bird, Alford, Scott Skiles, Bobby Plump, Rick Mount or Jimmy Rayl — has been — or may ever be — as popular as Damon Bailey.

He lived in the limelight of national attention from junior high until he left Indiana University. Through it all he remained unchanged, amiable, soft-spoken and modest, yet proud. And his roots remain as deeply imbedded in Lawrence County as the limestone for which it is noted. He will forever be part of the lore of the area.

His is a career that makes small towns proud. He is to his hometown of Heltonville what Dick Farley was to Winslow, Don Buse and Gene Tormohlen were to Holland, Gil Hodges to Petersburg, Bob Lochmueller to Elberfeld and the entire 1954 team to Milan.

Signs at the entrance to Winslow proclaim "Home of Dick Farley." Farley, now deceased, led the Winslow Eskimos to the Elite Eight of the state basketball championship and played on Indiana's 1953 NCAA title team. Welcome to Holland signs add, "Home of NBA stars Gene Tormohlen and Don Buse (an Indiana Pacers all-star)." A sculpture of Gil Hodges in the rotunda at the Pike County Courthouse at Petersburg notes his Major League Baseball accomplishments even though he was a star in basketball. Lochmueller led his Elberfeld team to its best season ever in 1945 before becoming a Louisville Cardinal star, professional player and an Indiana high school basketball coach with a 399-150 record. At Milan, a museum will soon house reminders of the 1954 team that won the state championship and became a model for the movie "Hoosiers."

Bailey's career is imbedded in a limestone tablet shaped like the state of Indiana and placed a few feet from the gymnasium at Heltonville where he learned the game and his father was the school's second leading scorer.

The marker, more than ten feet high, five feet wide and nine inches thick, is engraved with the highlights of his career and is accented at the top with a likeness of his face and at the bottom with gratitude from of citizens of

Heltonville. A $4,000 goal to finance the memorial was exceeded by $2,000.

It was a tribute not only for Damon's career on the basketball floors of America, but for his demeanor. He was the child every mother wanted her son to be, low key, unfazed by adoration, a role model even though he disdains that role for himself or other athletes.

And he remains a model for others to emulate. Katie Gearlds, Indiana Miss Basketball 2003 and Damonesque in play and demeanor, cited Damon in an interview with *The Indianapolis Star* after her team won the 3A girls state championship:

"I know a lot about Damon Bailey because I used to be a big I.U. fan (she will, however, attend Purdue). "I loved to watch him play and I remember him in the state championship game. He kept taking the ball to the basket and going to the free throw line to keep his team in the game.

"Our assistant coach Steve Cox kept saying, 'Remember Damon Bailey,' so during the game that's all I kept telling myself as I dribbled down the court, 'Damon Bailey, Damon Bailey.' "

Damon, however, remains more than anything a reminder of Hoosier values. He represents an era when young Hoosiers shot hoops on the sides of barns, played games in haymows and awaited the pairings for the state basketball tournament when there was but one class and a kid from Heltonville or Shawswick or Needmore could dream of beating Bedford in the sectional tournament.

A few youngsters still may be seen at the outdoor goal on the playground at Heltonville. But not as many or as often as Damon Bailey would like for it is there, in the small towns of the state, that Indiana became a synonym for basketball.

—Wendell Trogdon, who assisted Damon Bailey with his first book, Damon — Living a Dream, *is the author of 20 books. He is a retired managing editor and columnist for* The Indianapolis News, *which ceased publication after he retired. He is a native of Heltonville and now lives in Mooresville with his wife, Fabian.*

By BOB ADAMS

Hoosier fans from the northeast corner of the state had a lot to cheer about and a lot to ponder following the 1984-85 basketball season.

With Steve Alford and Uwe Blab leading the way, the Hoosiers opened the Big Ten season with a stunning 87-62 win over Michigan. By late February, the Hoosiers had fallen to 6-7 in league play, and archrival Purdue was on the docket.

Every Hoosier fan remembers that ball game. Upset with the officiating, coach Knight threw a chair across the floor. The Hoosiers didn't make the NCAA that season, but they were invited to the NIT, where they went to the final game before falling to UCLA and Reggie Miller.

Coach Knight, according to the local papers, had even sneaked away a couple of times during the season to follow the career of one Damon Bailey, an eighth-grader, for goodness sake, from some little place in southern Indiana called Heltonville.

We soon found out that Damon was making a name for himself in AAU circles, and was dunking the ball as an eighth-grader. Once, according to writer John Feinstein, in a fit of frustration, Knight said Damon could play for IU right there and then, and would be the best guard the Hoosiers could put on the floor.

Local interest in Damon picked up as he entered high school. When Damon scored 37 points against Chris Lawson's (himself an IU recruit) Bloomington South team, it earned a couple of paragraphs in the local papers in our area. Interest really picked up when Damon led his team to the state finals, where it would face a great Marion team led by Lyndon Jones and Jay Edwards.

Behind Jones and Edwards (also both IU recruits), the Giants were working on a historic three-peat, hoping to become the first team in the state to post back-to-back-to-back state championships for the first time since Franklin did it in the early 1920s.

It was really with a sense of relief that Decatur area fans were watching the state finals in 1987. Back in 1985, Bellmont, led by Kip Jones, won the South Adams sectional by an average of almost 25 points per game. The Braves then knocked off Peru by 30 points in the morning round of the Marion regional. This earned them the right to face the Giants in the finals. Back then Marion didn't lose very often on their home court, and they didn't that night either. The Braves played the Giants tough, but lost 87-78.

Two years later, the Braves had a new coach, Kevin Leising, and led by the Gross cousins, Luke and Scott, posted a school record 21 wins. They won the South Adams sectional, then beat Northfield in the regional opener, but once again had to face Marion at night.

After a bad first quarter, the Braves and the Giants played even the rest of the way, but once again Marion prevailed.

So, many fans from northeastern Indiana were rooting for freshman Damon Bailey and his Bedford North Lawrence Stars, but it wasn't to be. For many of us, this would be the first of many times we would catch Damon and crew in the state finals.

It was a great season for basketball in the state. IU won the NCAA. The movie "Hoosiers" (produced by Decatur native David Anspaugh) came out. And Damon was a year closer to enrolling at IU.

The following season, Damon would once again lead the Stars back to the state finals. Another North Central Conference team, Muncie Central, stood between them and a trip to the final game.

And, once again, there is no love lost between a lot of basketball fans from this part of the state and the Muncie Central Bearcats. For the second straight season, local fans had a one-game look at Damon, which is more than they had the following year when Damon's team lost in the regional to Pat Graham's Floyd Central team.

By committing to IU early, Damon's every move made the local news. His senior season, practically every game was reported in our newspaper. The IHSAA, making one of its few smart moves in the last couple of decades, moved the state finals to the 40,000-seat Hoosier Dome.

The lucky fans in attendance would be part of the largest crowd ever to witness a high school sporting event. For the unlucky ones, the games would be telecast statewide.

The Stars almost didn't make it to the final game. Unheralded William Moore scored 23 points in the first half, and the Stars trailed Southport at the half, 32-23. BNL did regain the lead by the end of the third quarter, and went on to win 58-55.

The final game served to only enhance the Damon Bailey legend. Down by six points with about two-and-a-half minutes remaining, Damon took over. Two minutes later,

Damon had scored 11 straight points, and the Stars claimed their first state title.

The story had an ending right out of the movies. Damon was named the Trester Award winner, and later, Mr. Basketball. Who else was there?

Damon had attracted some 40,000 fans to a high school basketball game. Thousands of others had watched it on television. After Damon graduated, attendance at the state finals declined dramatically. Who would have believed that some kid from some little town in southern Indiana could have had this much impact on the game?

Every IU ball game is televised in northeastern Indiana. Cable installations soared as IU fans had cable installed so they could watch Damon and the Hoosiers on ESPN.

The next four years went by way too quickly. Some games stick out — some vividly and some not so, but Damon always exhibited a lot of class. When it was learned his sister Courtney, had leukemia, hundreds, if not thousands of people from this area sent messages and prayed for her.

The legend continued to build over the next three years, then it was over. Coach Knight was quick to praise Damon. "For four years I have been Damon's biggest critic," Knight said, "but I have also been his biggest fan.

"Nobody could figure out what Damon should be — a guard, a forward, a center. What he was, was one hell of a basketball player."

When it was Damon's turn, he spoke about leaving practice many nights totally teed off (he used a more descriptive word). He called his sister Courtney down on the court to join him and said she had been his inspiration.

There were few dry eyes in Assembly Hall.

Damon never played NBA ball, even though he probably should have. He did join the Fort Wayne Fury for a few years, and even at that level he continued to draw crowds. When he left the team to play a few months in Europe, attendance at Fury games dropped dramatically.

Then, it was over. Damon decided it was time to go home, to retire from the pro game, and time to give his body a rest. Damon did this with the same class and style he had shown throughout his basketball career.

Damon's name is still magic in this part of the state. He holds a couple of basketball camps in the area, which sell out each year.

Like the Golden Age of Basketball during the 1950s, and single class basketball which ended following the 1996-97 season, the Damon Era is now a part of the Legacy that is Indiana High School basketball.

When I was a kid, I can remember grown-ups talking about Bobby Plump, and the "Miracle of Milan." When I was in grade school I remember Rick Jones, Glinder Torain, and Mike Rolf leading Muncie Central to a state championship in 1963.

Now that I have grandkids, I can tell them, "I have been watching Indiana High School Basketball, man and boy for over 40 years. Why, way back in 1990, I can remember when Damon Bailey took over the state championship game."

Such are the things from which legends arise.

—*Bob Adams, who lives in Decatur, is a past president of the Indiana High School Basketball Historical Society, the author of 19 basketball books and an Adams County sports writer and radio commentator.*

BY ROB BROWN

My perspective of Damon Bailey comes from my role as the Fort Wayne Fury's public relations director, radio announcer and as Damon's roommate when the team played on the road.

I joined the Fury in July, 1995, and Damon reported to training camp in early November that year, a few days after he was cut by the Pacers.

That 1995-96 season was a pivotal one for the Fury. The franchise was in its fifth season and the novelty of having a team was beginning to wear off for Fort Wayne fans. After leading the league in attendance for the franchise's first two seasons, the team dipped to seventh in the league in 1994-95. That promising season crashed with a 4-14 finish and the team slogged through the final month with a ragtag roster.

Damon's arrival proved to be a shot in the arm for the club. We opened the season with an 11-point loss in Quad City and faced them in a rematch in Fort Wayne the following night. We had a near sellout crowd of more than 8,200 fans and I remember the crowd hanging on Damon's every shot. He missed his first four or five shots, but I still recall the explosion of the crowd when he finally hit his first bucket and I can see Damon backpedaling on defense with his hands up in an "it's about time" fashion.

The team struggled through a difficult November and December but gathered momentum through January and February. Once March arrived, the team caught fire and won eight of twelve games and five in a row to finish the season. Because the standings in the CBA were based on the quarter point system, we still had to win the last quarter of

him about that misfortune. He returned to the Fury that day, played that night and scored 30 points in a victory over a good Rockford team. It was a win the team needed after getting drilled by Quad City two nights earlier.

Perhaps the thing that typifies Damon's stint in Fort Wayne was the final two months of the 1998-99 season. Even though he had been cut by Cleveland, he never talked about the unfortunate timing of the injury that cost him a final chance to play in the NBA. He continued to play without complaints through the aches and pains, never taking a night off and continuing to do what he could to help the team win.

My lasting impression of Damon as a player will not be the big plays he made or his impact in the victories the Fury won. It will be of an early January game in Florida during his second season with the Fury. Damon had eaten some bad seafood the night before and spent the entire day of the game alternating between his hotel bed and the bathroom. As his roommate and as someone who saw him throughout the day, I didn't think there was any way he could possibly play that night, but he did.

—Rob Brown is the assistant director of communications for the Los Angeles Clippers in the National Basketball Association. He was the Fort Wayne Fury's public relations director, radio announcer and Damon's roommate on the road during CBA Games.

Other Comments

JAY FRYE, an owner of Fort Wayne Fury during Damon's years with the team and a Kripsy Kreme business partner with Damon. Among other things, he now runs a summer basketball camp in Florida with former NBA big men Robert Parrish and Clifford Ray:

"Damon is one of the classiest people I've had a chance to know. It is a tragedy he is not in the NBA. He earned his way there. After his third year with us I think he had developed into the best point guard in the league. It is unfortunate the time was not right and he didn't get a call-up in time.

"It should have been a great story — him coming here (to Fort Wayne) and developing himself. He did all that but never got the call because teams made terrible judgments on him. I tried with many teams to get him an opportunity but it did not come at the right time. Cleveland did have him at a training camp but never gave him an opportunity to play.

"He was, however, a great story for our team and he helped the franchise a great deal as a player and as a person and he had a positive effect, of course, on the attendance as did Keith Smart.

"It was great watching Damon's family — mom and dad, grandparents, Uncle Phil — come to every home game. It was a great experience for me to have a chance to spend some time with him and his family and get to know them.

"It is sad it didn't end up the way it should have with Damon in the NBA. Damon did help a couple of guys get great opportunities. One of them, Moochie Norris, was called up by the Houston Rockets and signed a long-term $22.4 million contract.

"I have bought the rights back for a team here in Fort Wayne, but it would be hard to operate a team without Damon because he was so much a part of it before. He was what the CBA was all about, players getting opportunities."

DAN BUSH, who coached each of Bailey's four years at Bedford North Lawrence, including the 1990 state championship team and the 1990 Indiana all-star team:

"Damon was a great basketball player who always has been a class individual. He still is that same person. Nothing has changed about him despite all that he has accomplished. He remains the same Damon we've always known.

"He seems to be a happy young man in his role as a husband, as a father and as an owner of a business. He is a devoted husband and a devoted father, one who loves and cares for his kids. He was the baby-sitter for his three youngsters, taking a week off from work, when his wife had surgery. It was a new experience for him and he handled it well as he does all things.

"I see him at most of the BNL basketball games and we run into each other around Bedford from time to time so we still keep in contact. He has lived up to the expectations — as high as they were — that we had for him."

JACK BUTCHER, Indiana's winningest high school coach with 806 victories, all at Loogootee High School from where he graduated:

"Damon's success can be attributed to a personal commitment on his part to do more than what was required. His achievements showed an unwavering commitment to hard work, dedication and an exemplary attitude.

"During Damon's high school career, he was without a doubt a drawing card which helped to pack the gyms wherever he played. However, I feel Damon's greatest and lasting contribution was the positive influence he had on the young people who saw him play and observed his persona."

MORRIS "MO" McHONE, former CBA coach and coach of the 1999 USA Pan-Am basketball team on which Damon Bailey played. McHone is now an assistant coach with the Los Angeles Clippers.

"At one stretch when he played at Fort Wayne, Damon was probably one of the three or four best players in the CBA. He could really shoot the ball, was extremely smart and was probably a better point guard than people gave him credit.

"I think we, as coaches in the CBA, sometimes misused him. He was such a good shooter that you would automatically put him at the two (shooting guard spot), to take advantage of that. He was tough to guard.

"He should have made the NBA. I still, to this day, do not know why he did not.

"In the 1999 Pan-Am games, I had a chance to coach him instead of coaching against him. It was then I learned how much pressure he put on himself. I thought he played well at those games, but I had the feeling that he could have played better if he had relaxed a little bit.

"I think the perception of Damon by NBA teams was that he was a little slow. I think that was wrong. I think the fact that he was such a good scorer may have kept him from being envisioned as a point guard or a set-up guy. Again, I think that was wrong.

"In the CBA your scoring always come from your guards. It's a guard league and your point guards always score more than they would in the NBA.

"He wanted to make an NBA team, especially Indiana, but there wasn't an opportunity there. It is all about going to the right team where there's a need for you.

"You hear that when players graduated after playing at Indiana for Bob Knight they are burned out. I am not sure but that may have happened with Damon. I don't know that during the summers he was willing to put in the total effort that it took — the weight training and all that — because he was so relieved to be away from the situation.

"Being an Indiana kid and being the No. 1 player carries a lot of pressure, especially in those days under Coach Knight. Such a player carries so much pressure everywhere he goes, every day of his life. I think Damon was happy to get away from all that. Sometimes, I felt that he didn't really want to strive to get there (top status) again because he knew he didn't want to go through that pressure again.

"As a person, I thought he would be a rich man someday. He was, in my opinion, way ahead of his time as far as knowing how to make money and how to keep the perspective of what pro basketball is all about. Even as a young guy, you could tell he was well grounded. He didn't get into things haphazardly. My impression of him was that he was a very intelligent person, more intelligent in handling and making money than the average Joe."

*   *   *

In the pages that follow, Damon updates — in his own words — his career since he left Indiana University and offers thoughts about his roles as a husband, father, businessman and basketball fan. He provides insight on coach Bob Knight and the fear factor under which his players perform, gives his impression of the professional game and reveals his thoughts on business, politics and parenthood as he looks to the future.

DAMON TODAY

"A family is a perpetual source of encouragement, advocacy, assurance, and emotional refueling that empowers a child to venture with confidence into the greater world and to become all that he can be."

—Marianne E. Neifert, U.S. pediatrician, professor and author.

FAMILY FIRST

It has been said basketball demands loyalty and responsibility and gives back fulfillment and peace.

This is true. I have found, however, that being a husband, father and businessman demand that same loyalty and responsibility and yield even greater returns. Each brings fulfillment, each a sense of pride and inner peace.

For me, the roar of crowds has been replaced by the laughter of our children. The joy of competition now comes in winning a contract over a rival. The thrill of victory comes with success in business.

Much has happened since my first book, *Damon - Living A Dream*. In the eight years since, I have spent time with the Indiana Pacers, played for the Fort Wayne Fury in the Continental Basketball Association, been on a professional team in France, participated on the USA team in Pan-Am competition and become fully involved in business.

More importantly, Stacey, my bride in 1995, and I have become the parents of three children. Alexa was born in 1996, Loren in 1998 and son Brayton in 2000. They have become the focal point of our lives as they should be and we are grateful each of them is healthy and happy.

The three of them have given me a better understanding and appreciation and even more respect for what my parents, Wendell and Beverly, did for me. I never realized until Alexa, Loren and Brayton were born how hard it is to be a good parent. Each deserves the time and attention that my schedule sometimes makes difficult to give them.

Damon, Stacey, Brayton, Alexa and Loren
at Disney World 2003

My mom and dad put the priorities of my sister, Courtney, and myself ahead of their own. The sacrifices they made were greater than I had thought until I became a parent. It was a responsibility that was a wake-up call for me. I have to help run a business and earn an income, yet make room for my wife and children.

Just being at home is important. If your son or daughter wants help with homework, to play around with the basketball or baseball or go to a dance class — whatever — you need to be there, or at least as often as possible.

My parents were almost always there for me, be it an AAU, high school or college game, often arriving home after midnight and rising the next morning to be at work on time. They attended many CBA games and visited us when I played in France. That support meant a lot to me at the time. It means more to me today now that I am a parent.

I catch myself asking my children if I can wait until tomorrow or some other time to read them a book. I constantly have to tell myself they come first even after I have worked all day and want to sit down to read the newspaper or watch a game on TV.

That was one reason I quit playing in 1999. I needed to give more time not only to Stacey but Alexa and later on Loren and Brayton. They missed my presence when I wasn't home. That made me understand I could not — and did not want to — take the time needed to become the player I wanted to be to compete at that level.

I had done that since grade school, whether it meant getting up early each morning to stay in shape or to work on my game. I realized I no longer could play each season, yet devote time to both my business and my family. The priorities of my life had changed.

From a selfish standpoint I would have liked to continue to play, but it was not the best choice to make.

Life is a series of choices and the wisest decisions are not always the easiest to make. My wife and children had become more important in life than continuing my basketball career. If life was only about playing games, I would still be playing.

Basketball takes a lot of time and it would have required even more if I was to advance to the NBA level I had wanted. It would have meant more time away from my family and business.

My two daughters, as I noted, were bothered by my absence when I was on road trips and the time I was away at practice. Aware of that, retirement from the game was an easy choice to make.

At one time being a professional player was my most important goal. It no longer was. It was time to put aside some of my personal desires and to follow the role my parents had played for me.

I would be remiss if I did not express my gratitude to my wife Stacey, who has been my sweetheart since high school. She has supported me through all these years, allowed me to spend the time it took to practice for and play basketball in high school, college and at the professional level.

She has taken care of our home and children and is understanding when business commitments take me away from home for long hours and at night on occasions.

She is a great wife and mother, who sacrifices her own interests to allow me to be successful in business as I was in basketball.

I have never forgotten what coach John Wooden told me when I visited him in Los Angeles with my agent, Bill Sweek, who played for coach Wooden. As we were getting ready to leave, coach Wooden asked me about my family. When I finished, he told me, "The greatest gift you can give your children is to love their mother with all your heart."

That is what I have tried — and will continue — to do.

Being a father is the toughest job I have ever had, tougher than anything I have ever done or likely ever will. I do not think I was a selfish player, but it required a certain degree of selfishness for me to accomplish what I was able to do. There were times when I had to put basketball or business ahead of everything — Stacey, Mom and Dad, friends, or just being able to enjoy myself as did other young people.

Now I want to do what my parents did for me. Yet it is very hard for me, not because I do not want to but because of my background and work ethic. I realize both my family and business require my time and attention. Sometimes I catch myself thinking that the business is the priority and that Stacey can take care of the family.

That conflict, I think, comes because I had put myself first, as many men do, to achieve personal goals. We accomplish objectives because our parents relinquished their time and their own interests. I did not realize until Stacey and I had children what my parents had given up so I could succeed in basketball and in life. It means a lot more to me today, even though it meant a lot to me ten years ago.

Our lives, as with most young families, are hectic with busy schedules. Stacey is the Bedford North Lawrence cheerleader coach, Alexa is in school and she and Loren attend gymnastics and dance classes. I sometimes work until 7 p.m. or have business meetings at night. So we often pass each other in the driveway.

When Stacey and I do have free days, we try to spend all of them with the children. We may play the "Candy Land" game, read books to them or just sit and talk. We enjoy taking them to the movies or out for pizza or to restaurants. The girls are well-behaved at restaurants and with most groups, something they learned when I was playing at Fort Wayne and we went out for most of our meals. Brayton is learning, but he is still young. Sure, they may not always behave as perfectly as we would want them to, but they have to be exposed to different circumstances and taught good behavior, not left to learn on their own.

All that aside, I want to be good person in the eyes of my wife and my children. If I can be seen in that way, all other successes — be they in business or whatever — will be secondary. I cannot earn the right to be so judged if I put myself or the business ahead of them.

A parent gets but one chance to raise each child and it needs to be done right. You can't go back and do it again. If I am successful it will be my greatest achievement, more important than athletic awards or championship trophies.

When I look at Alexa, Loren and Brayton, I recall what Grandma Case said during Stacey's first pregnancy: "You don't know what love is — you may think you love Stacey, your parents, your sister — until you have your own child. Once you do, you will realize what love really is."

She was right. I experienced that with each child. I realized the depth of that love when Loren was diagnosed with pulmonary hypertension at birth. Rushed to Riley Hospital in Indianapolis, her condition remained critical for almost two weeks. We waited, as we watched her almost lifeless sweetness. We were helpless; hope, prayer and faith in her doctors our only recourse.

It was sad and frustrating for I had — or so I thought — always been in control of my life, yet I could do little to help. Her condition changed suddenly one day and she recovered completely and remains healthy and active.

Riley Hospital is a great place where great things are done. It was there that my sister Courtney was treated for leukemia when she was a high school freshman in 1991. Like Loren, Courtney is in good health and leading a normal life.

She and her husband, Shane Nolan, who also is from Heltonville, are the parents of a son named Cade, who is a delight. The three of them joined us on a visit to Disney World over spring vacation in 2003.

BEYOND THE CHEERS

I am often asked if I miss the adulation of fans now that I no longer play and my name is seldom in the news. Others now revel in the limelight that once shined on me.

My answer is, "Not really." I am sure I would if it were totally gone, but I still receive some attention. Fans remind me of certain games, my impact on their lives, what I meant to Indiana basketball. I appreciate that. But that attention — being on the cover of sports magazines, being in the newspapers, being asked for autographs, having people greet you — is not why you play basketball or any other sport.

It is, however, something that makes you feel good and feel special. Too much of it can be burdensome as it was for me at times.

That attention has waned since I quit playing basketball, but some still remains, enough so that I do not miss the days when it was much greater.

For example I often eat at restaurants when I am visiting customers. Some days no one may know who I am. Other days, three or four people will stop me or come to my table and talk.

If no one ever came up to me and asked me about basketball or for an autograph again, I admit I would be bothered. In my case, basketball has been a part of my life since grade school.

Alexa remembers when I played. The other two don't recall that, but they are aware when I am asked for autographs and about my basketball career. I am sure they will face the scrutiny of fans when and if they become players in whatever sports they choose because they are my children.

THE PACERS

Chosen by the Indiana Pacers in the 1994 National Basketball Association draft, I signed a contract on September 23 of that year. The team soon ordered surgery on my knees to end pain that had bothered me since my sophomore year at Indiana University.

I resumed practice later that year, but remained on the injured reserve list for the entire season. I did manage to stay involved from the start as I progressed through therapy and rehabilitation. I made some road trips and did my "rehab" with the team trainers.

It was near the end of the season before I could work on my individual game, shooting, cutting and running. It wasn't until about the time the playoffs began that I could begin to compete. Unfortunately, at that stage in the season, teams seldom practice because most of the players are banged up and injured and resting their bodies for the remaining games.

I never played a regular-season game with the Pacers, but I learned a lot from coach Larry Brown and the team while with them.

As a rookie I went through the normal indoctrination under my "boss," Sam Mitchell, a true professional. It was an experience within itself. I carried bags into hotels for the veterans, brought donuts to practice and was often awakened from sound sleeps and ordered to fetch players soft drinks from vending machines.

It was something to which I was not accustomed. It is that way for all rookies and it is best not to buck the system if you want to make it through that first year. I survived that year and, despite that role, I enjoyed the experience and the knowledge I gained.

The next summer I played as a Pacer in the summer league and had another minor surgery on one knee. I attended training camp with the team that fall and played in exhibition games before I was cut just before the regular season started.

Those operations and my lack of play for almost a year restricted what I could do and, I think, led to my release.

Sure, I wish things had turned out differently, but I was grateful for having had that experience.

Some fans thought I might not have been treated fairly, but I was given an opportunity to make the team. I just wish it had been a longer opportunity under better circumstances. I had not had time to completely recover; neither my game nor my body were at the point they needed to be for me to perform as well as I could.

I did learn a lot about the professional game while I was with the Pacers. It helped to be around players like Reggie Miller, Byron Scott and Sam Mitchell. I learned a lot about the game, what the NBA is all about, by listening to and watching them.

They knew how to take care and not abuse their bodies, to make sure they got the rest they needed, what foods to eat and not eat, to refrain from excessive alcohol. Those are all things great players watch. Sure, there are bad apples as there are in any barrel. But the ones who are truly successful do things the right way, the way they are done by the Millers, Scotts and Mitchells.

Fans do not realize what players give up to compete in the NBA. They are paid a lot of money, but they forfeit some pleasures in order to stay the stars they become.

The three were class individuals. Reggie Miller is one of the nicest players in the game. He is both a competitor and an entertainer, who plays to the crowd. His so-called feud with movie director Spike Lee was staged in part by Reggie, the entertainer. He is on the court, of course, to win games, but he puts on a show at the same time and enjoys so-called rows with fans like Lee.

I played a lot of golf in the spring of my second season with Scott and Mitchell. As I said, they were great people as were Antonio Davis and his wife. The entire Pacer organization was — and is as far as I know — a group of quality individuals.

*   *   *

I am often asked if I was surprised when I was cut from the roster by the Pacers. Truth is, I was a little bit of everything. I was surprised, mad, sad, disappointed, a combination of these and other things.

I believed at that time, as I still do, that it was bad for me to be drafted by the Pacers, despite the enjoyment and learning experience I received from the experience. It put both the team and myself in bad situations.

Neither the team nor I could have delivered what fans would have wanted. I had been this Indiana idol, if you will, and fans had great expectations for me. I would never be a Michael Jordan, although I am sure I could have been a very good player at that level. Would I have been an Indiana Pacers star? I knew myself and my ability well enough to realize I would not be a Reggie Miller, but I could have made a contribution.

Some fans, no matter how good I might have been, would have expected the Pacers to play me every minute of every game. They would have criticized the coach and the organization had that not happened. It is how Hoosiers are toward popular athletes who grow up among them.

My injuries likely entered into the factors the Pacers considered when they released me. I think the decision to keep Fred Hoiberg instead of myself came after they realized neither of us would get much playing time that season. The team was good even then and very little contribution would have been expected from either of us.

It probably was easier for them to release me than have some fans resent the fact I was keeping a spot warm on the bench and not playing much. I do not blame the team for wanting to avoid that distraction.

I had played in Indiana my entire life, had been Mr. Basketball, an All-American at Indiana and enjoyed immeasurable fan support. To then be drafted by our home-state Pacers was a dream come true.

Looking back, I think it would have been better had I been drafted by another team. Being picked by the Pacers created more obstacles, it seemed, than advantages. I would not have faced such high expectations with another team.

I had a very good senior season at I.U. until I was hurt. That resulted in a decline in my statistics, which may have caused me to drop to the 44th spot in the NBA draft.

As with most organizations, there is political-type intrigue within the National Basketball Association. The superstars are at a completely different level than the average players. There were, and still are, players in the Continental Basketball Association and on other so-called minor league teams who are better than many NBA players who make up the sixth to twelfth spots on rosters.

Most of those NBA players remain in the league because they do not cause problems and are content with secondary roles. And more importantly, they may have agents who also represent the stars on the team as well. In a quid pro quo, those agents may agree to negotiate a huge contract for great players provided the team also signs average players for secondary roles.

I've played against a lot of players who are in those positions on NBA teams. They are good, but they are no better than dozens of other players who do not make it into the big time.

I would have liked to have played in the NBA to say that I did, to finalize all the work I put into the game. Disappointment is part of the game. It is a part of life. You deal with it, play the cards that are dealt and make the most of them.

Even if I had stuck with the Pacers, and all other things had gone as they have — family and business — I would be in the same position I am today. I do not think I would have wanted to put in the effort and time to do what needs to be done to remain in professional basketball.

I played basketball because I enjoyed it. It made no difference if it was shooting or dribbling by myself, with Dad or in the gym, I enjoyed the competition, working continuously to get better.

* * *

I did attend a Cleveland Cavaliers training camp in 1998, the year of the NBA lockout. The Cavaliers had three veteran guards, Derek Anderson, Brevin Knight and Wesley Person, so it was not a good fit for me. I was released before the start of the delayed NBA regular season and returned to the Fort Wayne Fury where I continued to play in the CBA.

FORT WAYNE FURY

I had been with the Fort Wayne team since 1996, joining the team immediately after leaving the Indiana Pacers.

It took me a half-season after I joined the team before I started feeling comfortable. I had not played a lot in competition since leaving I.U. and I had to learn the point guard position that I had seldom played. It was difficult for a time, but once I had recovered from my injuries and adapted to the new position I played much better. I was slowed for a time with a pulled cartilage, but those things happen and you live with them.

Admittedly, the first year there was not a good experience. I did not want to be there. No kid, me included, grows up wanting to play in the CBA or to have to go overseas to play. I am not sure I even knew there was a CBA until a short time before I went to Fort Wayne.

It took months, it seemed, for me to get into the flow of games and to feel comfortable. It was a frustrating period in my life and I was not sure at the time I could endure that first season.

It was a difficult time. The coach at the time and I didn't seem to mesh. It was a whole new world as far as travel was concerned, going from I.U. and the Pacers to the CBA. I was accustomed to first-class accommodations, private planes and five-star hotels. I was spoiled, I suppose. Suddenly I am riding on buses or flying commercially on 15 to 20-seat planes, praying we would reach our destination, then staying in low-end hotels. It was a dramatic difference.

It was a time when I asked myself, "Why am I doing this?" I was married, involved in business back in Bedford and could survive without the income. As I said, I really did not enjoy it. I didn't want to be there. I didn't like the coach and I wasn't comfortable playing for him. So, I did ask myself, "Why am I doing this?" a number of times. Eventually, however, I was happy I stayed with the team.

The CBA was not the NBA. The league played in places like Yakima, Washington, and in small cities in Connecticut, Florida and Louisiana as well as larger cities such as San Diego and Grand Rapids. It covered the nation and travel was often difficult.

Trips to Yakima were long, always adventures and not ones to anticipate with glee. We flew from Fort Wayne to either St. Louis or Chicago, then caught flights to Seattle where we boarded small planes barely big enough for the players and coaches.

The 140-mile trip southeast over mountains from Seattle to Yakima took about an hour and was rough, as in extremely rough. I don't get scared on many planes, but I admit I was frightened a couple of times on those flights. It didn't hurt my feelings at all when I no longer had to play in Yakima, a city of 62,000 people in south central Washington.

It made a big difference for me when Gerald Oliver became the Fury coach my second season there. He was enjoyable to be around and directed us on a great run to the playoffs before we reached the CBA finals. I was again enjoying the game and I was playing professional basketball, trying to improve enough to reach that next level.

The CBA, of course, was not where I wanted to play. Like every good player, I wanted to be in the NBA. I was named to the 1997-98 All-CBA first team, while ranking 3rd in the CBA with 7.3 assists per game. I was the conference player of the week three times during my time with the team.

You will read elsewhere that Jay Frye, an owner of the Fury, credits me with helping Moochie Norris reach the NBA and eventually signing a $22.5 million contract with the Houston Rockets.

When Moochie came to the Fury, I was the point guard and Carl Thomas played the Number 2 or shooting guard position. When Thomas moved up to the NBA, I moved over to his position so Moochie could play at point guard. I knew the league and how to be successful by then and I was able to help Moochie a lot. It worked out well.

We played well together and had long stretches when each of us had outstanding games. I helped him with some games, how to get the most out of his teammates and how to get along with them. He was a very talented player and I was happy he was able to prove to the NBA that he belonged in that league.

It was fortunate that the Fury had two owners, Frye and Jay Leonard, who did not make money their main objective. They wanted to be involved with the team, to make sure it was a good one and to do something for the good of Fort Wayne. They set a standard for owners of minor league teams, no matter the sport.

The team went through some trying times, then started to get players who were better people and easier to be around. When that happened, we jelled as a team under a new coach and went to the CBA finals the second year I was there.

Keith Smart, whose last-second shot gave Indiana its 1987 NCAA championship, came in later as a coach. He brought in quality players who were class individuals, accommodations got a lot better and so did the attitude of the team. In the four years I was there, the arenas became bigger and better and so did the hotels. Travel was still vexing at times, mainly because of the trips to Yakima.

The coliseum at Fort Wayne was one of the better arenas in the CBA. Early on some of the teams played in a high school gym or on college court at first, but all eventually had their own coliseum-type venues.

The level of play became very good and so were most of the players. Some were there because they had never been given a chance to play in the NBA; some because, to put it bluntly, they were not very good people. We had a few of those types on the Fury team for a time before coach Smart began to bring in quality people.

It was a good league when I left. Competition was better as was the level of play. Players were making some good money and I enjoyed the game. It was a big difference from the first year to the last.

*   *   *

It is too bad more players like Moochie Norris do not get an opportunity to play in the NBA. The ninth, tenth, eleventh and twelfth players on NBA teams were no better than the best CBA players. A Reggie Miller, a Tracy McGrady or a Kobe Bryant likely can't be found on a CBA team. A lot of good players can be spotted, however. Moochie Morris was one of them.

It is difficult to dislodge the role players on NBA teams. They know their roles, are good people, do not create problems, cause trouble or create embarrassment for their teams. They stay in shape and can step in and play when needed.

Once a player like that is established, there is no reason for a team to replace him with a player of equal talent. The coach and management know what they have and are reluctant to call up someone they know little about.

An example is Mark Madsen, a Stanford University graduate and former Mormon missionary, who is a back-up center to Shaquille O'Neal with the Los Angeles Lakers. Madsen gets little playing time, but likely works hard in practice, stays out of trouble and gives his maximum effort when called on to play.

He and other such players deserve to remain on NBA rosters. I think that hurt me and other CBA players. Call it the luck of the draw. It is a credit to those who are there. They have done what is expected of them and have not squandered the opporuntity. They aren't asked to be superstars and they do exactly what is expected of them.

The CBA was a great training ground for coaches and a stepping stone for players. At least four former CBA coaches held the top spot on National Basketball Association coaching staffs in 2002-2003 and another 29 former coaches and players were assistant coaches.

FRANCE

My experience as a player for the Pau-Ortez team in France in 1997 gave me an insight into European culture.

It was something I enjoyed, one of those places that is good to visit but not to live. We flew on charter flights and stayed in the nicest hotels, which even in France are not what they are in the USA.

First class by European standards is not the luxury it is here. It's like watching old black-and-white movies for much of the continent appears at least 20 years behind modern America.

The coaches who spoke English treated basketball as a job, so we practiced each morning and afternoon when we did not have games. The two two-hour practices in mid-season were a surprise and a big adjustment for an American player. The morning session was mostly spent on fundamentals and drills, which explains in part why foreign players like Vlade Divacs and Tony Kukoc are so skilled when they play in the U.S. They have worked on the basics day after day.

In the U.S. it is assumed players have acquired those talents before they reach the professional level. A lot of American players have not. In Europe, players work constantly to perfect the skills that too many Americans think, unfortunately, they already have.

A lot of players who get big bucks for playing in the USA do not want to spend too much time at practice, which may explain our lack of success in international competition.

The high level of basketball there was a shock to me. So was the support the team received from fans. We played in an 8,000-seat arena and it was packed every night with loyal — and very vocal — French fans. Play well and you are cheered loudly. Perform poorly or mess up and you are booed even louder, even if you are on their team.

An American on the team naturally becomes the target when the team isn't playing well. He may be performing better than anyone else, but he gets the criticism nevertheless. That adds to the pressure of an unfamiliar environment.

Pau is a city of 90,000 people in a metropolitan area of 140,000 residents, the largest in southwestern France. The arena where we played was the most spacious, modern basketball venue in Europe. The nearby areas are scenic with the snow-capped Pyrenees Mountains visible on sunny days.

The Pau-Ortez name came because the origin of the team was in Ortez, a smaller city about 20 miles away.

It was a good experience because my wife Stacey and daughter Alexa were with me in Pau and my parents were able to visit us for two weeks. Most of the young people we met spoke English which made the stay more enjoyable than if we had felt isolated and alone.

PAN-AM GAMES

It is a great honor to be chosen to play for your country no matter what level. I took pride in playing for the USA in the 1999 Pan-Am Games in Winnipeg which was special for me, especially because I had been unable to play for national teams on two other occasions when asked.

Naturally, I appreciated the chance which I saw as a reward for having worked hard much of my life in order to merit a selection to the team.

Our Pan-Am coach was Morris (Mo) McHone, who as coach of the Sioux Falls Skyforce always had one of the best teams in the league and won CBA titles in 1995 and 1996. Keith Smart, my last coach at Fort Wayne, was one of his assistant coaches during the games.

The CBA didn't have too many teams and we played each other so many times we got to know opposing players both on and off the floor. We appreciated each other's talents which added to the pleasure of being on the same team even during Pan-Am practices in Los Angeles.

The team was made up of the best of the best of the CBA and from a basketball standpoint that is ideal. It is always good to compete with and against the strongest competition, even in practices.

Each player on the 12-man team deserved to be there, yet understood he was a part of a team and realized only so many shots can be taken and playing time would be limited because each man on the roster was a star on his own team.

The team was unselfish and each player wanted to win. We had a lot of very smart players who understood the importance of the games from a national perspective and were willing to give up any personal glory to win. We were playing for our country, we wanted to win and I was happy I was able to average 10 point in the five games.

We won the silver medal, losing to Brazil in the final game. The international game was different for us as the NBA stars have learned from the Olympics. That international style is more like the way basketball should be played than what the NBA plays. The NBA has too many rules and regulations that limit what teams can do. Foreign players learn to — and continue — to play basketball as we knew it at the high school and college level.

Basketball is still basketball in college. At the professional level it is played from an entertainment standpoint. That's why the USA is struggling in international competition.

The foreign teams can play against a zone defense or use one themselves. The players may not be as talented or as athletic as our guys but they are wiser both from a basketball and a fundamental standpoint.

That leads me to wonder why some of our players, the best in the NBA, are reluctant to play on our national teams. I can't understand why they decline to give up their summers in order to play for their nation. It is a chance to prove how good they are and to honor their country at the same time.

My experience on that Pan-Am team was very good despite that loss in the championship game. It was something I can tell my kids about when they get old enough to understand.

AFTERTHOUGHTS

Once a player reaches the Big Ten level, basketball becomes similar to a job. You are not paid outright, but you receive an education for your efforts. In return you are expected to perform and help your team win games. It becomes a business as well as a game.

I won't debate here whether that is right or wrong but that is the way it is. It takes a lot of fun out of basketball as I'm sure it does other sports. Players want to prove in college they are better than their teammates to gain attention and a spot on a professional team.

It gets worse at professional levels where there is big money to be earned. Players become more competitive within the framework of the team. Instead of working together to win a championship as they had in high school, they are competing with teammates for playing time, for a contract and for exorbitant salaries.

I was concerned with winning more than anything else. That desire likely hindered my professional progress. Winning had been preached to me from the first to last game I played. I remain proud of the fact that at every level I played — every team I played on — our teams were winners. I hope I was a part on each team's success.

Was that best for me individually? Looking back, it was not. I learned that unselfishness can be a deterrent to individual success.

I played for a lot of years getting other players involved in the game and doing whatever needed to be done to help my teams win. Sometimes that meant scoring points, sometimes it meant getting rebounds, sometimes playing solid defense. Whatever it was, I tried to do it from game to game, season to season.

Most players have to be selfish to get attention from professional teams, to be more concerned about self than the team, and to pay more attention to individual statistics and personal glory than winning.

I've always felt that if you win games the recognition will come. At the higher levels of the sport that is not the case. Winning almost seems secondary to a lot of players. As long as they perform well it doesn't matter what the team does.

It is difficult to get that attention on professional teams when every player is a standout and most are accustomed to scoring 20 to 30 points a game. There is just one basketball and a limited amount of time. I recall one game with the Fury where three of us scored a combined 75 points. When that happens other players do not get a lot of chances to score. Not everyone can play every minute and shoot 15 to 20 times a game. That is difficult in the CBA where it is obvious every player wants to move up to the NBA. Each feels the best way to get there is to score 25 to 30 points a game. When you have 10 to 12 players on a team who are trying to do that it makes winning secondary.

That selfishness is a byproduct of the game and seen as necessary by players who want to move up. Personal goals become more important than team goals and the game suffers.

BURNOUT

I did feel some basketball burnout the last two or so years I played. It was more like a job than a sport, but I did enjoy the games and the competition. If all I had to do was show up at 7 p.m. and play, sure I would be there. I would still be competing.

That, however, cannot be done at the CBA or NBA level. A lot of preparation and a lot of conditioning and practice are required. Those last two years were a struggle, especially in the summers. I would work all day, then go home to spend two or three hours running, lifting weights, playing basketball and whatever else it took to be in shape.

That burden had started to a degree back at I.U. It was fun at I.U. at times. It was not fun and I did not enjoy it on occasions when it seemed liked a job and coach Knight was on a tirade for some reason or another.

Even had I stayed with the Pacers, I likely would have made the same decision to retire after the 1999 season.

It was the best thing for my family, the business and myself.

I look at my career as a success, but I am not totally satisfied with the results. I think every player thinks he could have had a better career. I could have worked harder at times to make myself a better player as Larry Bird did.

Teams I was on won the Indiana high school basketball championship, two Indiana-Kentucky all-star games, a Big Ten title and reached the Final Four of the NCAA tournament. I was a part of one of the most successful four-year eras ever at I.U. and a member of the university's all-century team.

Those are things I will remember.

OUR CAMPS

Our annual Damon Bailey basketball camps allow me to give something back to the game that has meant so much to me.

One of the reasons I conduct camps each summer is to attempt to help offset what I see as a decline in the quality of basketball played in Indiana today.

Fundamentals of the game seem to have been forgotten as more and more players seek ways to make spectacular dunks and snazzy passes. That is why my camps stress the fundamentals of the game every great player needs to learn.

We obviously have to run contests and conduct games that are fun for the kids. But 75 percent of the time is spent on fundamentals in order to make each participant better. We teach the correct way to pass, shoot, dribble, set screens, rebound, move without the ball; all the things that are important to become good team players.

We also talk about desire, dedication and determination in general. Each of those attributes will be needed later in life, be it as a wife or husband or in basketball, law, medicine, education, business or any other endeavor.

We have 18 week-long camps around the state of Indiana each summer that attract an average of 100 to 150 boys and girls. Students are divided by ages into sections.

We have two basic objectives. One is for the kids to enjoy the camps and have fun while learning. The other is for parents to feel they have received a full return for the money it costs them.

I want a child who comes to camp on Monday to learn how to be a better player by Friday and to comprehend some things he or she can work on the rest of the summer. The unfortunate thing is that in one week — and I tell the kids that — they will not see a great improvement in their games between Monday and Friday. That just cannot happen in five days. No camp can promise — or do — that.

But what we hope to do is give them a lot of information in those five days where they know what it takes to be a good player and ways to help them become good. It is then up to them. It makes little difference how badly their parents want them to be good. What really matters is how hard they want to work.

Others can encourage someone to be better and work with them to improve, but the child is the only person who can make himself or herself great. He or she is the one who has to be on the driveway at home or in a gymnasium sharpening individual skills.

We can talk all day about dribbling, but the youngster has to practice dribbling. We can show him how to shoot but he has to be the one who practices shooting, shot after shot, day after day.

Fundamentals are something he cannot work on for a week, then go on to something else. They have to be practiced daily or at least on a consistent schedule. If a player can hit 10 straight free throws, that is good, but it is better if he shoots until he hits 20 of 20, 50 of 50 or 95 of 100.

Goals are often too low. Anyone who plays a lot can eventually hit 10 of 10 alone in a driveway and think that is good enough. It is not. To do that in a hostile environment is much more difficult and can only be done through diligent and continual practice.

I may not get the best players at my camps, but that is not important. We stress the same points to each, whether the participant is already good or has never played.

And students who want to be good should attend a summer basketball camp. Some players in our age group think their abilities are beyond the need to attend camps, that they don't need a Damon Bailey, a Steve Alford or a Billy Keller to teach them how to shoot. They think they already are good at it.

The truth is, they likely are not. Sure, they can shoot a basketball and hit more shots than another fifth grader. If they had been taught by great shooters they could become a lot better. Rather than being the best in their grade or community, they might develop into the best shooter in the state or the nation.

Camps can point out their weaknesses, show them how to improve their strengths and teach them fundamentals of the game they have yet to learn.

Too many players would rather reach a certain level and think they have achieved their objective. It takes time to put in the extra time and effort to go beyond that and become even better. It is too easy to be satisfied with lesser goals than it is to work to become Mr. or Miss Basketball in Indiana or to become a leader of a championship team.

The camps for me are fun. It is a way for me to give back in the summers to the children of parents who have supported me. It is a way for me to help Indiana basketball, which I do not think is as good as it was five to ten years ago.

The first thing I do after greeting the players at each camp is to emphasize the importance of learning how to listen — whether that be to mom and dad, teachers or coaches.

We spend the first half of each day working on fundamentals, passing, shooting, rebounding, in groups of seven to 10. It is important for each kid to pay attention.

The only way they can get better in my camp is to listen. Neither we nor high school coaches have the time to walk each participant through every detail. Those who do not listen or listen but do not hear will not learn, so it is important to pay attention and try to grasp what we teach.

Our staff includes Indiana University players like Tom Coverdale, Kyle Hornsby, Jeff Newton, A.J. Moye and George Leach, plus some former high school standouts. We spend the first half of each day working with groups of seven to ten on passing, shooting and rebounding.

The appearance of those I.U. players make our camps that much more special for many of the participants. Most of our older kids know who they are and what they have accomplished as individuals and as a team.

If the campers had their way, we would scrimmage and play team basketball the entire day. To keep them happy we do finish each day with contests and games which give us some indication of what they have absorbed.

We teach screening, for example, on the first day of camp, then observe them in five-on-five games at the end of the day. The first day in those games, the kids show no indications they have heard a word we said about setting screens. By the last day of the camp, however, they are doing that.

The same goes for the other fundamentals we have taught. It makes me and the counselors feel good to know what we have been trying to teach has been learned and is being done in the right way.

That is important. If the campers do things the right way on the playground or in the driveway they will continue to improve.

We also try to stress the importance of basketball intelligence, the need for players to think for themselves for it appears too many young players do not understand the game. Many seem to play in robotic mode, to act rather than react, to do precisely what they have been told. Coaches may mention what to do in a game situation, but it does not always mean a player should not think for himself. A coach, for example, may say to make this cut, but if another cut allows an opening to the basket it should be made. No coach will complain if you do that. Rules like that are guidelines, not written in stone. They require decisions on the court.

Basketball requires basketball smarts. More players need to learn to develop and use that intelligence on the court.

A lot of our campers return year after year. I have some who have come to my camp from the second grade through their freshmen years. It makes me feel good to know they have confidence in what we teach.

We develop a relationship with many of them after three or four years. Some of the counselors will trade email messages or letters with campers throughout the winter.

Two former Indiana all-stars, Miss Basketball Sara Nord of Jeffersonville in 2000 and Cole Sinclair of Bedford

North Lawrence in 2001, attended our camps. We keep in touch with many players like that.

Those are among many ways in which I try to give something back to the game and play a role in the lives of young people. We may see up to 2,000 young people — both boys and girls — each summer.

What we do in those camps, I think, is important. I would like each of the participants to realize his or her maximum potential in basketball. But I care even more that all of them become class individuals who lead quality lives.

That is why we also teach abstinence from drugs, alcohol or whatever hinders a person's ability and judgment as an individual, a husband and parent, an athlete, an employer or an employee. If we are able to reach one kid with something we do or say our summers have been well spent. That is what our camps are all about.

*   *   *

Editor's note: The Damon Bailey camps are among the Summit Camps organized and operated by Dave Carrington, a teacher at Garrett High School and a high school coach 17 years at three schools, Jac-Cen-Del, North Judson and Garrett.

He and Damon conducted camps sponsored by the Fort Wayne Fury in 1996 an 1997 and have operated the Damon Bailey Camps since then under Carrington's Summit Camps umbrella.

"It is Damon's presence," Carrington stresses, "that makes those camps different from others promoted with names of celebrities. It is the most frequent question I get, is Damon actually at the camps. He is at the camps, every day, all day. Few other celebrities can say that."

The camps deal with the basics, fundamentals every young player needs that are taught by Bailey and others who know the game.

"We have a staff that travels with us and we may add some local coaches, depending on the number of campers," Carrington says, and adds, "In 2002 and 2003 we added some Indiana University players with the cooperation of coach Mike Davis. Those players were excellent helpers who blended in well with the regular staff.

"Attendance at the camps have long-range benefits for participants from the fundamentals they learn and the motivation they receive just from being around Damon and the staff we have.

"The experience cannot be anything but positive."

* * *

Carrington and Bailey also work together to conduct a barnstorming tour around the state. In 2003, 15 games were conducted throughout northeastern, central and southern Indiana. Players included Bailey; I.U. seniors Tom Coverdale, Kyle Hornsby and Jeff Newton; Brad Borgman, a 1999 Indiana all-star from Jac-Cen-Del who played at Indiana University Southeast; and Josh Allen, who grew up in Heltonville and played at Bedford North Lawrence.

The competition was tough, including a game with the six graduating seniors from Butler University's 2003 NCAA Sweet Sixteen team.

BUSINESS

Instead of basketball my competition now comes from involvement with business ventures, the most important being the Hawkins Bailey Warehouse in Bedford.

Randy Hawkins and I formed the business almost on the spur of the moment in September 1994, three months after I graduated from I.U. I knew Randy from the basketball games he, my dad and other men played out at the Heltonville gym.

Randy was manager of the Hoosier Parts outlet in Bedford and hired me to work for the firm on summer vacations. I traveled with salesmen when they called on customers. It was interesting, enjoyable and competitive and I learned some of the ins and outs of the business.

Hoosier Parts was both a heavy duty maintenance supply company — which is what we do now — and an automotive firm like Napa or AutoZone. We planned only to concentrate on the heavy duty side and that is what we have done. If you want an oil filter for a small pickup you get that from an auto parts store. If you need one for a bulldozer or a heavy truck you can get it from us.

Hoosier Parts may have thought Randy had hired me so we could start our own business, but that was not the case. It was, as I said, impromptu and not something that had long been planned for I expected to be drafted by the NBA and play somewhere.

I had nothing to lose. Randy, on the other hand, had a good job with Hoosier Parts where he had worked for 15 or so years. We are more than just a warehouse in Bedford. We not only sell and deliver heavy duty maintenance products, we try to help firms get more service from their machines and help them with ways to do that.

Rather than duplicate all that Hoosier Parts did, we chose to concentrate on the heavy duty side of the business. We do not sell to individuals and we have very little retail business. We send salesmen out to obtain orders, then deliver the products our customers need. We deal with firms that have fleets of vehicles and machines whether they be trucks, school buses, construction equipment or mining machinery. We also sell to the industrial market such as factories and plants.

By doing that we can specialize, limit our inventory to seven or eight strong lines and have fewer manufacturers to represent. This allows us to get to know what we sell, then go out and help the customers with their problems. We do more than ask what a firm needs, then take it to them.

We stress the fact we help the customers get longer lives out of their engines and extend the time between oil changes and other maintenance. We try to provide them with products that will let them do that.

Firms can't make any money from a machine that is out of service. That is extremely important for a coal mine or construction firm that works 24 hours a day. The longer a firm can keep its machines at work the more profitable it is. An idle machine makes no money.

We do not want our companies to have breakdowns before they need us. We want to provide them with products that will keep their machines working 500 hours instead of 250 hours between service. We know if we give good service, the supplies we sell will be reordered from us time and again. We intend to keep those customers supplied with what they need when they need it, preventative maintenance products used in their shops on a regular basis.

We are not — and do not plan to be — a company that has something for everyone. We wanted our own niche in the market, then capitalize on it. We have been able to do that.

By concentrating on this market we can limit our inventory and deal with a select number of manufacturers. We started with seven or eight strong lines and specialized in them so we could really get to know the products we were selling. That allowed us to help the customers with whatever problems they might have, not just to ask what they need and then take it to them.

We are able to help firms get longer life from their engines and to reduce the time the machinery is down for service. We show them procedures, explain the benefits from buying what we recommend.

It means a lot to a company if we can provide it with products that allows it to double the time between service for its equipment. The less down time means more production for the machinery and for employees. No one makes money when a truck, bulldozer or any other equipment is idle.

By tracking our inventory, we make sure the customer has the items needed when they need them. We know if we give good service, we will get reorders on a regular basis. We want to provide our customers with the items they need

Those are the types of things we do and it has been something we have stayed with for almost ten years. Oh, we have deviated from that somewhat, taken on a few new products. But we still do not want to be a company that has something for everyone.

The business has gone well. Randy and I were a good fit. His experience in the business helped. My name recognition was a benefit. That allowed us to have an entry into some businesses that we might not have had otherwise.

Sure, we have differences but we each are open-minded enough to consider each other's views and reach an agreement.

We have grown tremendously and now have 15 employees and ten pickup trucks and delivery vans. Our warehouse is stocked with supplies that can be delivered when — or before — our customers need them. We, like almost every firm, noticed the economic slowdown in late 2002, but that was a leveling-off in sales, not a reduction. We did have to work hard to maintain that level, but we have great employees whom we appreciate. We demand a lot out of them, but we try to reward them for their efforts. As owners we care about them as people as well as employees and I think they will continue to care about us.

I'm on the road at least once a week, sometimes two or three days. It depends. When we decided to sell in the Louisville market in 2002, I spent three or four days each week, knocking on doors with our salesmen.

Once we have those customers, it is vital that we continue to keep that personal contact. As we have grown, it has become harder to do that but we do it as often as we can. Those contacts give us a sense of reality of what is going on in the market. It is easy for me to sit behind a desk and give suggestions to our sales force. We cannot offer advice to our salesmen if we do not know what they face, what our competition is, or how our customers feel about us.

It's like any other business. Managers who stay in the office get comfortable and sometimes go through the motions of the daily routine. Change is constant and we have to know the market and the territory, have communications with our customers and let them know we appreciate their business. After all, they have given us an opportunity to serve them. It is up to us not to squander the chance to have an impact on their company.

They have shown they trust our company to provide them with what they need. We do not want to break that trust.

Other companies have comparable products, but service is one thing that we can control. I can help make sure we take care of the customer better than our competition.

We try to hang our hats on those things in which we can excel. Our customers may be able to go across the street to buy what we are selling, but our intent is to serve them well, sell them quality products and make them like us better than the competition.

Fleet of Hawkins Bailey Warehouse delivery trucks

Having a part in that business made it easier for me to give up a career in basketball. It is something I knew I would like and I have not been disappointed. It is the type of work I like and I would not have been happy had I chosen to stay home all day or spent most of my time playing golf.

Business, like basketball, is competitive. It has its highs and lows. You may pick up a big account one day, lose another the next, or have to defend one against a rival firm the third. There is nothing we do that some other firm can't offer. We are service oriented and we try to take care of our customers, be it from making deliveries to informing them of what we have available for them.

It doesn't bother me to get up and come to work. We are open from 7 a.m. to 5 p.m. and I am here from when we open until we close on days I am not on the road. In addition, we often have business contacts at night. We have employees who work longer hours on a fairly regular basis. We do what it takes to get the job done and that includes myself and Randy.

A lot of travel is involved as I have said, but very little of it requires overnight stays. Some of our customers are four hours away which means I am on the road eight hours in addition to the time spent with them.

Working here daily has been a challenge that has allowed me to draw from the competitiveness I learned in basketball. Each day brought — and still does — something new and like in basketball we have to deal with rivals who are bigger, stronger and more experienced. We had to devise strategies that would overcome those disadvantages and make us better than they were.

Instead of physical capabilities and game experience, the game of business takes more mental effort. I still, however, use the three Ds — dedication, desire and determination — of basketball today.

It has been a great opportunity and something I knew would provide me an income and a career without basketball. We had the business that was doing well and provided me an income even when I was playing in the CBA. I continued to play because I truly enjoyed the competition and had goals I had not accomplished, not because I needed the money.

That aside, the fame, whatever others choose to call it, has definitely had a positive influence on our business. I'm sure there have been instances where my reputation gave us an opportunity, an entry, we might not otherwise have had. Once we have that edge we have to perform and meet the customer's needs. Fame no longer is enough. We have to deliver what we promise.

We want to be very good on our own merit, which is why we try extremely hard to be best at what we do. Once we get in the door we can provide a service to the customer and help make each company we deal with more profitable. To do that we supply good products at competitive prices, listen to their problems and help them find solutions.

I think that is our success. Once our name recognition gives us an edge, we make the most of the opportunities

I work very hard at the business as does Randy. I put a lot of time into it both mentally in the office and physically out on the road calling on customers and contacting people. One thing I can control is how hard I work and how hard our people work to take care of those we serve.

As I have said, it is a business I enjoy. It is an elixir as great as basketball. The thrill comes not from cutting down nets or receiving trophies; it comes from doing the job well and in meeting the needs of customers. And, of course, being successful at it.

LIFE WITH KNIGHT

My Choice

There was never much doubt that I would attend Indiana University once I graduated from high school. Growing

Coach Knight (left) at BNL game

up 20 minutes away from I.U. as a Hoosiers fan I knew I would accept a tender to play basketball there if given the opportunity.

I did try to keep an open mind and look at other schools but I had dreamed of playing at Assembly Hall. I think that I.U. was confident I would accept its offer and did not recruit me in the

71

same manner it would have other players it wanted. It did not do a big selling job, because that is what recruiting is, a sales job.

There was never a lot of conversation between us (neither with coach Knight nor the assistants). It was a situation where I knew they were interested in me because both the coach and his assistants came to a lot of our Bedford North Lawrence games. I did attend a few I.U. games at their invitation and talked with the coaches in the locker room.

So the way I was recruited was unlike it was for most players. The staff realized I was already sold on I.U. and did not give me the usual sales pitch. I agreed to attend Indiana at the start of the BNL season my junior year.

Even before that I think most other colleges realized that I was headed for I.U. I was contacted by a number of schools, but most soon assumed I would become a Hoosier upon graduation from high school.

Knight The Coach

Bob Knight, to borrow part of a Winston Churchill quote, is "a riddle wrapped in a mystery inside an enigma."

The coach is a complex contradiction, who demands respect but gives little in return. He is controlling of others, yet resents the authority of his superiors. He is rude, but expects others to be polite. He wants others to work to correct their imperfections, but makes little effort to amend his faults.

Sure, there is a lot of good about coach. In contrast there is a lot of bad. That explains my own contradictions about him. He is a great coach, but he is not a person to emulate.

My feelings about him are somewhat conflicted. A part of who and what he is about, a part of what he does and says is very good. In contrast I do not agree with a part of what he says and what he does.

In retrospect, I think that conflict within me led me to join some other former players to protest Knight's ouster as I.U. coach in 2000. I had been a part of his program for four years and felt, I think, a bit of loyalty to him as I suspect the others did. Indiana was losing a coach who had won three national championships and built one of the nation's top programs so it was natural to question a change.

Looking back on that day, I think coach's time at Indiana had passed. It was time for a change, to move ahead under a new coach who would be more attuned to the players of today, who would not be tied to the past.

That rally outside Assembly Hall was probably a misguided, impromptu spur of the moment reaction that should have been given more forethought.

I don't think any players can tell you that playing for coach Knight was enjoyable. I can't say all my time under Knight was miserable, but I also cannot honestly say it was always a good experience.

My feelings about him are very mixed. I did learn some things from him that have helped me and I use every day. Then again there are some things that could have been handled differently.

Fear was a factor when playing for coach Knight. That fear, that dread, was present every day from the start to the end of every season and sometime in between. Fear, rather than the sheer joy of winning games or a championship, was our motivation. I think that was the feeling of each of us who played at the time.

From a personal standpoint, the fear he instills in his players makes it difficult for them to play as well as they can. Basketball should be enjoyable and games should be fun.

Players respect him as a coach. They did when I played and I think they do now. None of us doubted his knowledge as a coach. But does every player like him? No. I don't think any player while we were there had a good relationship with him.

He was constantly on players. If he was on you one day, he would be on someone else the next. When it came to wrath he was an equal opportunity provider. No one was immune.

There was not a player there who at one time or another was not a recipient of one of his outbursts.

We each knew what all the other players were going through. We dealt with it together. As I noted, we tried to win games out of fear, not for the joy of victory over Purdue or other teams, which should have been our motivation. Coach got on certain players more than others because he knew they had stronger personalities and could handle whatever he might say. Others, he knew, might be crushed by criticism that severe. He often got on certain players in an effort to make a point to another player or to the entire team, knowing the person or players for whom it was intended would get the message.

That happened a lot, to Matt Nover in particular. Nover was mentally strong and mature and could handle whatever Knight spewed in his direction. That meant the coach often used him as a target in order to reach the entire team. Not many players in their teens could cope with that as well as Nover managed.

Can players compensate for all that criticism? You had your own unit within the team. You couldn't go talk to anyone outside the team, not your mom and dad, your high school coach or a buddy. They don't understand what you go through. You can talk all you want, but little alleviates the pressure.

Someone once audio taped a 5-minute tirade by the coach at practice that was passed around Bloomington and much of the state via the Internet. Laced with obscenities, it may have been comical to those outside the program who listened. It was not for the players who had to live with it every day, maybe not every day, but all too frequently.

People who giggled about it may have taken Knight's outburst as comical, which it likely was to anyone who was not at Assembly Hall at the time the episode was taped. It certainly was not humorous to the 10 to 12 players who had to hear similar diatribes day after day.

One incident is somewhat anecdotal now but I doubt if we laughed out loud at the time. In happened on the plane when we were en route home from a Big Ten game, Minnesota I think it was.

Knight had chosen Eric Anderson to be his target, literally, that night. He had thought Anderson had played poorly and as usual did not make his point and be done with the issue. He continued to voice his displeasure.

I was next to Anderson in the back seat of the team plane, which seats about 20 passengers. Knight was up front as usual, very seldom associating with players on trips. All of a sudden he picks up the fruit basket nearby and starts throwing the contents — bananas, apples, oranges and grapes as I recall — toward Anderson. These are not friendly, playful lobs. Knight is irate, his verbal volleys as numerous as his fruit fastballs.

He is calling Eric every name he can think of, none of which is complimentary, as we try to dodge the assault which may have been heavier than Knight ever observed by cadets in training at West Point.

Knight finally calms down, takes his seat, then gets up five minutes later and resumes his criticism. As he rants he grabs the emptied fruit bowl, walks back toward us and starts picking up these bits and pieces of fruit that had exploded during the bombardment.

As he does this he uses his favorite four letter word a few times as he blames Anderson for causing him to launch the attack. "I'm down here (expletive deleted) picking up this (expletive deleted) stuff because of you."

Knight seldom accepted blame for what happened. As in this case, he refused to recognize the fruit was splattered and he was picking it up because he — and no one else — had thrown it. There were numerous incidents like that over my four years there. He hated to lose, it seemed, because of what fans and critics might say about him. I don't know how many times he told players, "You are not going to do this to me or you are not going to do that to me," indicating they were doing so to harm him.

He had the attitude that when we played badly it made him look bad. A frequent question to players after a loss was basically, "Do you know what that makes me look like?" Our loss reflected on him, or so he thought.

Knight sometimes held grudges. He didn't erase the board once a game ended. If we had a bad game, he didn't forget it overnight. Greg Graham and I were relegated to the second five after we failed to live up to the coach's expectation in a loss to Kentucky.

We took out our setbacks, beating the new starters in practice and irritating Knight with our output. That wasn't enough to please the coach and neither of us, as I recall, started our first two Big Ten games. Once we entered those two games as reserves we were the most productive I.U. players on the court.

We had a mentality of anger because he had benched us. We probably made it a point to go out and practice and play harder than anyone else once the games started. That incident left me with mixed emotions. If we would have had the same mentality in the Kentucky game we might have won.

I think that is an indication that players get beat down under Knight's system. I think there are very few players who can play for him a full season — or a full career — as well as they can because of the mental strain. I don't know what it is like under different coaches because I didn't play for them. But sitting back from a distance now, it seems other coaches find different ways to motivate players. They sometimes have better results because they are not as mentally tough on players as coach Knight is.

I noticed a player at Texas Tech who was benched by Knight for one game, came back the next and had a super game. He won Knight's praise. The coach got immediate results. But that player will not be mentally strong enough to go through that in days to come. He just can't do it. People aren't strong enough to cope with all the highs and lows and the emotional roller coaster you are on with Knight. You just can't deal with it. You need something that is more level.

Consider these incidents, documented not by me but the Associated Press, that reflect the roller coaster that was Indiana basketball under Knight:

1974-75 — Tossed a writer from *Basketball Weekly* out of the locker room (which was his prerogative.)

1975-76 — Upset over two turnovers, Knight grabbed sophomore Jim Wisman by the jersey and jerked him into his seat. Wisman later said Knight was right in his actions, but Knight said he was wrong.

1976-77 — Rich Valavicius and Mike Miday quit the team and publicly criticized Knight.

1977-78 — Walked in on a party where marijuana was being smoked. He suspended five players and kicked three players off the team. (It was one incident that few people criticized.)

1979-80 — Was charged, and later tried and convicted in absentia, for hitting a Puerto Rican police officer before a practice at the Pan-American Games. Knight was sentenced to six months in jail but the government of Puerto Rico decided in 1987 to drop efforts to extradite him.

1979-80 — Playfully fired a blank shot at *Louisville Courier-Journal* reporter Russ Brown, saying he did it to keep from going nuts. A week later, Knight and his wife took turns at the microphone and chided the Assembly Hall crowd for not cheering enough during a game against Northwestern.

1980-81 — Used his weekly program to show films of a "sucker punch" involving Isiah Thomas and Purdue's Roosevelt Barnes, which he said proved Thomas' innocence. Critical of the "Purdue mentality," he riled Boilermakers fans and officials by bringing a donkey wearing a Purdue cap onto his TV show. At the NCAA finals, a Louisiana fan claimed Knight stuffed him in a garbage can.

1981-82 — Knight denied he had cursed Ohio State guard Troy Taylor. Ohio State later supported Knight.

1982-83 — Critical of Big Ten officiating, Knight cursed Big Ten commissioner Wayne Duke. Knight later blasted officials for the "worst officiating" he had seen in 12 years.

1983-84 — Cursed Michigan coach Bill Frieder twice on court and once in a post-game news conference.

1984-85 — Tossed a chair across the court during a game against Purdue. Knight was ejected and suspended for one game. Knight made a formal apology.

1985-86 — Given a technical for shouting at the officials during a game against Illinois. He later kicked a megaphone and complained I.U. cheerleaders had disrupted a free throw attempt by Steve Alford.

1986-87 — Assessed a technical foul, Knight banged his fist on the scorer's table during an NCAA regional tournament game against LSU. The university was fined $10,000 by the NCAA and Knight was reprimanded.

1987-88 — Refused to let his team finish an exhibition game against the Soviet Union after he was ejected for arguing with a referee. He was later reprimanded by the university.

1988-89 — In an NBC interview in which Connie Chung asked how he handled stress, Knight replied, "I think that if rape is inevitable, relax and enjoy it." He explained he was talking about something beyond one's control, not the act of rape, but the remark triggered protests and a march by 300 people on the Indiana campus.

1990-91 — Asked not to be renominated to the Basketball Hall of Fame, calling the voters' rejection of him in

1987 a "slap in the face." He was inducted into the Hall in 1991.

1990-91 — Publicly feuded with Illinois coach Lou Henson, who called him a "classic bully" who thrives on intimidation.

1991-92 — Barred a female Associated Press reporter from the locker room, saying it was inappropriate for her to be there and also against university policy. All reporters were subsequently barred from the locker room.

1991-92 — After a loss to rival Purdue cost Indiana a share of the Big Ten championship, Knight canceled the annual team banquet.

1991-92 — The Cheaney bullwhip incident.

1993-94 — Suspended for one game after a sideline incident in a 101-82 victory over Notre Dame. During the outburst, Knight screamed at his son, Pat, and kicked him (probably unintentionally) in the leg. The coach then shouted a four-letter obscenity at fans who had booed his behavior.

1993-94 — In the Hoosiers' home finale against Wisconsin, Knight took the public address microphone and recited a profane verse directed at his critics.

1995-96 — The NCAA reprimanded Knight and fined Indiana $30,000 for Knight's outburst at a post-game news conference during the NCAA tournament. He had chewed out a media liaison for saying the coach would not appear at the press conference.

1997-98 — Knight was given three technical fouls in a home loss to Illinois. He called referee Ted Valentine's officiating the "greatest travesty" he had seen in 33 years as a college coach. Knight paid a $10,000 fine out of his own pocket to avoid a one-game suspension.

I cite these incidents not in judgment of the coach, but to point out the seeming constant distractions that Knight's behavior caused for the players. It was difficult to concentrate on basketball amid the conflict that surrounded the program.

As I mentioned, coach Knight is two extremes separated by an enigma. He goes from one end of the spectrum to the opposite end. There is no in between. That makes it difficult especially for an 18 or 19-year-old student to deal with that and attended class, too.

There was almost always controversy surrounding Knight and that filtered down to the team. The conflict is about the coach, but it affects the team and it is mentally hard on the players.

Coach Knight often doesn't realize or care that some of his actions are detrimental to himself and the image of his team. An example was the incident during the 1992 NCAA regional at Albuquerque, New Mexico, when he playfully used a bullwhip on Calbert Cheaney, a black player. It may have been fun for the coach, but it is doubtful if viewers across the nation saw much humor in the pictures they saw.

Several black leaders said they were offended. Knight denied any racial connotations to the prank and noted the bullwhip he used was given to him by the players, including Cheaney. Once again he shifted the blame even though it was his decision to use the whip.

Sure you have peaks and valleys with other coaches but the ups and downs are not as continual. For coach Knight, there was no middle ground. Things were at an extreme, either great or terrible. Players need a middle ground. I think there are different ways to motivate players to play hard and to play well.

As I mentioned, fear is a constant factor. It remains with you even after you leave. I had no casual conversations with him as a player and he was not one to banter with on trips. The only non-basketball talk I recall having with him as a student came when my sister Courtney was hospitalized with leukemia. He was compassionate at that time.

I never felt at ease around the coach. I do not think I would feel comfortable around him today. He didn't want to have a relationship with his players when I was there and I don't need to have one with him now. I knew if he wanted to see me when I was a player it would be to criticize my play, so it was good when you did not have to see him.

I can think of but a part of one season that was more pleasurable than stressful. As a junior we had great players who played well. We went 17-1 in the Big Ten and all was well. The coach once again was a genius to fans and observers; everyone was saying how great he was and he appreciated the accolades. He was in a good mood much of the time.

We rarely talked after I graduated. I had quit playing for the Fury when the coach called our house one morning over Christmas vacation. Stacey woke me up, said Knight was on the phone and my first thought, even at age 27 or 28, was an automatic, "Oh my, what did I do wrong?" I don't think I was scared, but it may have been a programmed reaction before I thought, "What do I care what he wants?"

He was demanding as usual, saying something like, "Bailey, we have practice at 2 o'clock. You need to be up here."

So I went up and we talked before practice. He said it was time for me to get back into Indiana basketball by attending some games and practices. I really hadn't done that, not because I didn't want to, but because I had been tied up with my own business and basketball career.

Coach Knight had mentioned a couple of times when I was at I.U. that he thought I did not have a good relationship with my dad, that he was too hard on me growing up. I never understood it then and paid little attention to the comment, thinking coach Knight was just being coach Knight. He again raised the issue without ever explaining what he meant. As I mentioned in my first book, I respect my dad more than any other man and appreciate all the things he and my mother have done for me. If either my mom or dad was "too hard" on me it was for my own benefit.

That may be an example of Knight in his control mode. He was a very egotistical person. I don't think I ever took time — until after he was fired — to really take the time to reflect on that or to realize that.

Coach Knight demands respect, and he demands it absolutely, not only from his current players but his former players. I think they respected him then, I think they do now. I know I respected him as a coach and still do. I just do not agree with how he does it.

He is there, however, for former players if they need help in finding a job, admission to medical or law school or whatever. I am sure that is why some former players have gone to him as a friend for that purpose. I can't say in my case whether he would have done that or not for I have never had to ask him for a favor.

I think it bugs him when a former player doesn't need his help. I didn't need him. I kept doing things with my life in basketball and beyond. I was an owner of a business and didn't really need his help the way some other players have turned to him.

The reported rift he and Steve Alford had — before they seemed to have reconciled in the summer of 2002 — may have been because Steve hadn't asked for help. I think that bothers the coach when he no longer has a big role in the lives of his former players.

He is a very controlling person, obviously from a coaching standpoint, but also as an individual. I think he likes — he enjoys — the fact that players need him, whether it is while having him as a coach or after they leave. I think he gets a thrill from helping a person find a job or improve his life. I think that pleasure comes, not entirely for the wrong reasons, but partly for the wrong reasons. It may be his ego or a desire to exert control and perhaps have former players beholden to him as they were when he extended them scholarships.

Knight is said to be somewhat resentful of some former associates who have remained as a part of the I.U. program. His son, Pat, an assistant coach at Texas Tech, seems to resent that some of his dad's former players attend practices under current coach Mike Davis.

Knight no longer is close with some of his one-time defenders, not because they have taken a stand against him, but because they have remained at I.U. He has seemed to turn his back on them.

His attitude has cost him some close friendships. One former associate who wrote him after his dismissal expressed his thanks for the time they had spent together and wished him well. He waited a long time for a response and when a letter came it was generic in nature, especially for someone who had befriended him and spent a lot of time with him.

It is a sad thing when you can't have a relationship with a coach, one where a player or even a colleague can feel comfortable talking to him.

So from that standpoint I don't need to see him or form a friendship with him. That aside, I wish it wasn't like that. Any other coach I ever had — from grade school to the professional level — was not like that. I was always free to talk with them about any problem I might have or to just carry on a conversation.

I admit I did learn a lot — some directly, some indirectly — from Knight. I learned accomplishment takes effort. It takes hard work. One has to dedicate a part of one's life to what he or she chooses to do. Work is required, little is given.

I learned indirectly how to treat and, more importantly, how not to treat subordinates. I want our employees to feel free to talk with me at any time about business or about themselves. I want them to enjoy their jobs and to work in order to succeed, not because it is demanded. I do not want them to work out of fear, which does not make a good employer or a good employee.

I do not think any one player can explain Knight's behavior in a way that it can be understood. I can't think personally of an experience that is comparable. Some people say it's like being in the military. I've never been in the service, so I don't know. It is, as I noted in *Damon - Living A Dream*, "like climbing a mountain, walking a tightrope or bungee jumping."

That is Coach Knight's way. Always has been, probably will always be to a certain extent. It has worked for him and given him success. He has won 800-plus games and winning is what he is concerned about.

He does appear to have mellowed somewhat and I think that is because of son Patrick. Patrick knows what players go through playing for his dad, understands the pressure they are under and is still young enough to relate to their problems. That is good, because Knight's system is even tougher on kids today than it was a decade ago. Society has changed. The world is different and so are players. They are becoming less likely to tolerate domination by a coach and less apt to play the little mind games that have been a part of Knight's system. They may choose the road when Knight demands "my way or the highway."

As long as he has players who can adapt to his style of play and do what he wants his teams will be good. He does know the game of basketball as well or better than any one else.

I think all his former players, even Neil Reed, who alleged he was choked by Knight at I.U., and Nick Valdez, who quit the Texas Tech team in mid-season 2002-2003, would say good things about his knowledge of the game. Knight is definitely a great coach, but there are a lot of other great coaches today from whom players can learn.

Knight is consumed to a fault with winning. To be competitive is good, but he is competitive to the extreme. I really believe when things do not go well he gets into a mind set that is out of his control. He does things that once done he wished he hadn't. By then it is too late.

I did see Knight grab players. And I have seen the so-called Neil Reed video tape and I do not think it was an appropriate thing to do. But I do not believe coach Knight had any intentions of hurting Reed.

I just don't think Knight takes into consideration at the time what it does to a young man mentally and emotionally. He acts on the spur of the moment. Grabbing Jim Wisman, grabbing a player's jersey is not something that is premeditated. He forgets that he is dealing with teen-agers who are not accustomed to being mistreated or verbally abused.

Despite the Knight regimen, the frustration and the fear factor that went with it, I do think I am stronger because of it. I think I am better prepared for the roadblocks and pressures that adults face because of what I went through with coach Knight.

I regret the coach told an *Inside Sports* writer after I left that he got less out of me than anyone he ever coached. I am not sure exactly what he meant, whether I did not live up to my ability or whether he did not do what needed to be done to get the most from the talent I had. That remark was complicated by the send-off he gave me on senior day back in 1994 when he called me "one hell of a player" and made other positives comments.

Contradictions like that make for a conflicted opinion of coach Knight. I had been there for four years, played hard, did what I could to help the team win. It is a sad thing for a player to endure what he has to put up with, then leave and have to deal with a comment like that.

It was a shame to have given someone four years of your life then learn he has made a statement like that. It says a lot about him, whether he was sincere or not.

As I mentioned at the start of this chapter, I have mixed feelings about Bob Knight. Does the good outweigh the bad? That is for each person who deals with him to decide. The answer is not easy. He makes for complicated situations. He is a complicated person. He is indeed a riddle wrapped in an enigma.

Other Coaches

I learned a lot about basketball — and life — from every coach I had from the AAU to the professional level.

Keith Smart, who is remembered for his shot that gave Indiana its 1987 championship, could coach as well as he could play. As a player he was one of my favorites when he played for the Hoosiers. I enjoyed playing for him with the Fort Wayne Fury. He had just retired from the game himself and understood what players went through.

Smart, like Dan Bush at Bedford North Lawrence, was a player's coach. Bush was extremely knowledgeable and he could adapt to the talent he had. Before I entered BNL, he had good teams that won with a controlled slow-tempo style. The Stars didn't blow opponents out of gyms, but no one could shellac them either. That was the style those teams had to play to win.

That changed when I was there and he had a different group of players. He opened up the game more and we played a more up-tempo game than did previous teams. He was willing to change styles of play for a game, for a season or for the talent he had on the team.

Unlike with Bob Knight, it was not his way, his style of play, or the highway.

And he listened to players and considered their suggestions. He was the coach, but he listened. He might not accept what we suggested or he might veto the idea. He could put his foot down when discipline was needed and no one doubted who was the coach.

He had his way of coaching. Bob Knight had his. Both were successful with the approaches they used.

Larry Brown, the Pacers coach when I was with the team, also knew how to treat his players. He did tend to act like Knight at times, yet he had the respect of players. It was business once practice started because he was there to see that the team improved. Once a practice or game ended, his demeanor changed and he joined in repartee with the players.

He took suggestions from players and he was friends with them. He is proof a coach doesn't have to be a 24/7 tyrant to be successful.

The approaches used by Smart, Bush and Brown created a more enjoyable atmosphere than was possible under Knight. I do not think anyone played out of fear under them, except for fear of how little playing time he might get or dread that he might be cut from the team.

I felt at ease with each of them and could talk with each of them whenever I needed.

Coach Mike Davis

It was good to see the 2001-2002 team advance to the final game of the NCAA tournament. It meant a lot to Indiana basketball, the school and to Hoosier fans, especially coming in the aftermath of Bob Knight's dismissal and the turmoil that followed.

Even though Knight had been gone a year, his supporters remained. Some were adamant. They no longer supported Indiana basketball or coach Mike Davis, just because he had replaced Knight. It would have made no difference who was his successor. Those Knight loyalists would claim that team two years later was "Knight's team," even though most of the players including upperclassmen had been recruited by Davis.

It was different for fans who had straddled the fence over the Knight ouster. They waited, willing to be convinced the change might be for the better, even if the coach who had maintained Indiana's position as one of the top basketball programs in the nation for more than 20 years was no longer there. That dramatic tournament run by the Hoosiers in 2002 convinced those open-minded fans that Indiana remained a power.

Whether die-hard Knight backers ever replace their Texas Tech hats with an I.U. logo remains to be seen.

No matter what fans thought of the coaching change, it was good for the program when Davis showed he and his Hoosier teams could maintain the Indiana tradition. It was important for Indiana basketball. It was important for the psyche of the fans, the university and the state. It showed that the program was bigger than one man or any controversy that surrounded him.

Coach Davis is intelligent and is surrounded by good assistants. The program will continue to succeed. Indiana basketball is Indiana basketball. It is the sum of a lot of people, not just one person.

It is, however, much different under Mike Davis. The Bob Knight way has passed. The atmosphere has changed; players enjoy the practices and the competition. The players are more relaxed, so are the assistant coaches. The fear is gone, but not the desire to win.

The gap between the coach and the players has narrowed dramatically. The change is obvious when you talk with players like Tom Coverdale and Kyle Hornsby, who were there under Knight. They were more at ease in their senior year even though the team's Big Ten record (2002-2003) of 9-7 was mediocre for a Hoosier squad.

Players feel free to talk and to banter with coach Davis, something no one did when I was there as a player. It was that relationship that helped make the team's drive to the 2002 NCAA championship game even more delightful.

It was so much different than what it was under coach Knight. It is like what basketball should be. It is, of course, always better to win. It is even better to do so in a pleasant atmosphere.

Coach Davis, like coach Knight, can, however, be his own worst enemy at times. He at times lets his emotional outbursts make him appear out of control. He blames others, not himself, for losses, giving his critics even more ammunition to use in their verbal assaults.

His comments that his team "just doesn't listen to me" after the 2003 NCAA loss to Pittsburgh added to the chorus of skeptics who consider him a whiner. He blamed "outside influences," be they the media, fans or friends for his team's loss. He called the team "selfish."

The following day he apologized, admitting he was a "sore loser," and explained, "I was upset and I was disappointed. But my boys know me and they know that I'm a little too honest sometimes. It is an area I need to improve on as a coach."

It was a refrain of his eruption after the regular season loss to Kentucky and on other occasions.

In fairness to Davis, I think it should be pointed out that he is under tremendous pressure. An observer can almost see the strain he puts on himself. He wants to succeed, to prove he indeed can replace a Hall of Fame coach

and continue to keep Indiana among the top basketball programs in the nation.

He had not encountered a level playing field from the
start. It did not help that he had been a Knight assistant
and a Knight supporter. That made him a target of both
Knight proponents and opponents. And it made it difficult
for him to give the team a new identity while facing intense
scrutiny.

I think that will change, once he shelves those
post-game outbursts, realizes criticism is part of the game,
shares the blame for his teams' losses and realizes he need
not be intimidated by the shadow of Bob Knight.

As Terry Clapacs, interim (now permanent) I.U. athletic
director, noted, "Sometimes coach Davis says things he later
regrets, but I still think he is a terrific basketball coach."

When Davis became coach, he sent letters to all the former players whether or not they agreed or disagreed with
Knight's dismissal. In the letter he told us we were welcome
at practices as well as games. He realized that Indiana University basketball is a family and made sure none of us felt
isolated from the team regardless of how we felt about
coach Knight. It was a very smart move on his part.

Every former player has helped build the I.U. program
to the level it is today. It is the obligation of each of us to
help keep it there. That is why I drive up to practice and
talk to the players and attend as many home games as I can.

There are few Indiana kids on the team today, so I think
if former players talk to the team we can help make them
realize the significance of Indiana basketball to the people
of the state. We can emphasize the rivalry that exists with
teams like Purdue and Kentucky.

I think each day coach Davis gets a better grasp on what Indiana basketball is all about. He is a "foreigner," so to speak, to some Hoosiers, even though he was a coach under Knight for a few years. Indiana basketball goes back 100 years and the tradition runs deep for both players and fans.

It takes someone new to the state, be it a coach or a player, a while to learn that.

A number of the players are not from Indiana or products of our high schools. People say coach Davis needs to recruit Indiana kids, but there is a reason he does not. Neither Indiana high school players nor Indiana basketball teams are as good as they once were in comparison with those from some other states. Only a few of the Indiana kids today are good enough to play Indiana University basketball.

Sure, you have certain players like Sean May, who got away. But that has always happened. Eric Montross got away in 1990. Overall the talent level of basketball here is not good enough to provide Indiana with championship teams.

That means a coach or recruiter has to go to Texas, Louisiana or somewhere else to find the talent needed to compete in the Big Ten. When you do that you have players who are unaware of the rivalry with Purdue or Kentucky. A game with the Boilermakers doesn't mean any more to them than one with Minnesota or whomever.

Bracey Wright, who is from Texas, didn't grow up hating Purdue or Kentucky. He probably grew up hating Oklahoma. Kyle Hornsby likely grew up detesting a rival of Louisiana State. The Indiana-Purdue game means little to players from elsewhere, at least the first couple of years they are at I.U. It is just another game to them.

But an I.U.-Purdue game, as we all know, is not just another game to Hoosiers. It is certainly not just another game to Indiana University or its fans.

I don't think coach Davis understood that at first. I think he understands it better each day.

Coach Davis, as do fans, would like more Hoosier recruits, but there are not many players in Indiana high schools who can compete with the cream of the crop in other states. Indiana once had the premier high school players in the nation. No longer. States, especially those with large cities where basketball is a way of life, produce better talent than we do today. So I don't blame coach Davis. To compete at the level of competition Indiana plays he needs players from outside Indiana.

High school recruits of the 1990s like me, Greg Graham, Calbert Cheaney, Alan Henderson and Pat Graham are not found in Indiana as they once were.

You need the top Division 1 players in order to win at Indiana, which is why Davis has had to look elsewhere. He has to search out the best players he can find wherever that takes him. He is doing what he has to do. But when he does that it changes what I.U. basketball has been in the past.

Players from out of state did not grow up watching I.U. basketball. It meant nothing to them until they were recruited to come here. Bracey Wright may know who I am now, but I am sure he wasn't aware of who I was when he came to the campus. He may have heard my name or that of other ex-Indiana players but I am sure he didn't watch I.U. games on television until he decided to come here to play.

Players like Wright and others from outside the Midwest don't know — until they get here — what it is like to get ripped by Purdue fans after a loss or be the target of boos when they step on the court at Kentucky. It takes a while for them to learn that those are not your normal games.

I grew up watching Randy Wittman, Isiah Thomas, Ray Tolbert and others play at I.U. in the 1980s. It is doubtful if Bracey Wright ever watched A. J. Guyton play when he was here in the late 1990s.

Players from outside Indiana have a different viewpoint than those who grew up here. That makes it important for former players to stay involved and to help keep Indiana at a high level. We can do that by stressing what the game means here and make recruits aware of the traditions and the expectations. We can help out of state players understand that victories over Purdue and Kentucky are important as are Big Ten championships and NCAA championships.

It was easy for the fans — and the players — no matter where they were from to love the team in 2002. It reached the championship game of the NCAA tournament and Indiana was back near the top of the basketball world. The team did not do as well in 2003 so the fact that only two players from Indiana get much playing time is a topic of conversation.

That is a part of the blame-game among some fans. They are sure to say Indiana would not have lost to Kentucky or Purdue and would have done better in the Big Ten if Davis had recruited more Indiana players.

The level of high school play in the state may improve in a few years. Right now I see no Bracey Wrights in the state unless it is someone whose talent is yet to be seen.

You will recall that Bob Knight had started recruiting more and more players from outside Indiana. Kyle Hornsby and Jeff Newton were not from Indiana. Neither was A. J. Guyton, Eric Anderson and a number of other players on Knight's teams his last few years here.

To compete with your competition you obviously have to find players who can do that. That is why recruiting has become national, even international. Look at all the college players who are products of foreign high schools.

So, to repeat myself, I think former players should continue to talk to the current squads and help players from outside Indiana realize the significance of Indiana basketball to the people of the state. We can emphasize the rivalry that exists with teams like Purdue and Kentucky and explain that in Indiana basketball is a way of life, not just a game.

Damon Bailey in a pre-dawn practice at Heltonville gym

HB WAREHOUSE
R #11 BOX 1192
BEOFORD, IN.
47421

31792-15

Customer's Order No. _DARREN_

DATE _SEPT. 1_ 19_94_

SOLD TO _JLS INC._

ADDRESS _EVANSVILLE   OWEN MINE_

SALESMAN _KANDY_   TERMS _NET 30_

CASH	CHARGE	C. O. D.	PAID OUT	RETD. MDSE.	RECD. ON ACCT.

QUAN.	DESCRIPTION	PRICE	AMOUNT
1500	4024B bxy 10W BLUE HYDRAULIC		
1500	1580B " DIESELALL PLUS 15W40		
1500	3930B " TRANS C30		
1000	3950B " TRANS C50		
-1000	3021B " 80W90		

ALL Claims and Returned Goods MUST Be Accompanied By This Bill

SIGNATURE _____

PITTSBURGH SALESBOOK CO., PITTSBURGH, PA. 15203

First sales order for Hawkins Bailey Warehouse

Stacey and Damon Bailey
at 1995 wedding

Damon with son and daughters at Disney World

Brayton, Alexa and Loren Bailey pose for camera

Damon soars for a Fort Wayne Fury basket

The 1999 USA Pan-Am team, Damon (center row one)

Damon at induction into I.U.'s All-Century Team

THAT SPECIAL SEASON

"High school basketball is pure. That's fun. Once you play college ball at an Indiana, a Kentucky or a North Carolina, or you play professionally, that's a job. You happen to get an education, but you are there to play basketball, I don't care what anybody says.

"My four years as a Bedford North Lawrence player was definitely one of the most enjoyable times of my life. It is the highest level of what basketball is meant to be."

I said that some time ago and I still believe it.

The rearview mirror into the past has given me greater appreciation of what our Bedford North Lawrence team did that night 13 years ago in the Hoosier Dome in Indianapolis.

The 1990 state championship remains special to me. I am proud to have been a part of it and I am sure I will be forever. The switch later to class basketball has made that one-class championship even more meaningful. It meant our team was the best in Indiana and that no other school — as is now the case with four class champions — could claim it was better.

It is good to know our feat remains stored in the minds of fans. Almost daily someone I meet recalls our run to the championship or mentions what our team meant to them.

We had great coaches, great players, great team unity. The fact we each had to work very hard to accomplish what we had set out to do made the championship even more special.

Even though we were a large school, some fans doubted BNL could compete with teams from metropolitan schools. We were considered a small town school with players from

Damon (second from right), teammates honored for state title

rural hamlets that would win a lot of games, but not against teams from Indianapolis or along the northern border of the state. We could not compete against what our doubters called "the big boys," even though we had reached the Final Four in 1987 and 1988 and had played well each time. To overcome those critics and win the state title was an indescribable thrill.

Our hard work had paid off. We played in the summer, three or four days a week, driving to Bloomington at times to play against college students, or against grown men on pickup teams at Heltonville or Oolitic. We learned from those adults, who were stronger and taller than us. They made us better and more competitive. It was that kind of competition that led to our success in the winter ahead.

High school players today no longer have that advantage. They play in open gyms and against teams their own age. Adults, some of whom became disenchanted with Indiana high school basketball with the advent of multi-class tournaments, no longer are willing to play on hot summer nights.

A lot of players today would rather do other things or they fear burnout if they spend too much time in gymnasiums. Some coaches discourage such competition for fear their best players will be injured.

Those things may be true, but they are excuses, not valid reasons and they keep kids from being the best players they can be. It takes time beyond open gyms in the summer and practices in the winter for players to develop as individuals and as a team.

It is in summer that players learn all the small things that it takes to be good, whether that be in individual workouts or playing against competition that is bigger and

better. Those older players force you to extend yourself to
new limits and to become a better player.

Kids today do not do that. The opportunities are not
available, mainly because consolidations have reduced the
number of men who played basketball in high school and
still want to compete in pick-up games. And if the opportunities did exist, I doubt that many young players would
compete. Many of them are interested in other endeavors,
some of which are not as wholesome as basketball.

As I have said, it is in the summers that players become
better whether it is at basketball, football or any other
sport.

Those 35 to 40-year-old men we played against made us
do things we were not used to doing and they required us to
become better in order to beat them. In the end it helped us
defeat some great teams, including Southport and Concord
in the state finals.

They gave us the trophy that March night in 1990 to
the cheers of 41,046 fans. In reality, however, we won the
championship on those sweltering nights when we scrim-
maged against men at gyms in Heltonville and Oolitic.

Had we not done what we did we would not have been
successful.

It was an accomplishment which all of us — the
coaches, the players, managers and trainers — still savor. It
brought pride to residents of Bedford, Heltonville, Oolitic,
Shawswick, Williams, Tunnelton, Fayetteville, Needmore,
Springville and rural areas of Lawrence County.

A consolidation that had merged what had once been
nine basketball teams into one had finally — after 16 years
— become a school of one. The old rivalries of the past were
forgotten at last. Fans from small cities and towns around

the state considered us their team. They appreciated our rural roots and the effort we had extended to be winners despite the odds we faced and the doubts of our skeptics.

We were too close to it at the time to really appreciate what we had accomplished. The anticipation of my freshman year in college and I.U. basketball occupied much of my mind. As did my teammates, we had our youth to live and new goals to reach.

BASKETBALL TODAY

What's Wrong?

Most fans agree that Indiana high school basketball no longer is among the best in the nation. Sure, teams like Pike are outstanding year after year, but the enthusiasm and the support has waned dramatically.

Fans no longer crowd gymnasiums, seats remain vacant at state championship games, local teams no longer are topics of conversation at barber shops or corner restaurants.

Many hoops have disappeared from home driveways. Goals in parks remain unused. Many athletes have turned to soccer or other sports for competition.

Into the late 1900s Hoosiers went to high school games on Friday and Saturday nights. It was a way of life. It was part of our culture. We had done it forever, moms and dads did, it is what their parents had done. It is disappointing to see empty bleachers at games, especially during tournaments when tickets once were at a premium.

The decline started with school consolidations. No longer did each boy in a school have a chance to make the team so fewer parents went to games to see their sons play. Heated rivalries between small towns ended and many fans of abandoned high schools chose not to support the new consolidated teams.

I was delighted our BNL teams offset that trend and made fans throughout the school district feel they were a part of our achievement.

The change to a multi-class tournament has sapped the interest of both players and fans. Small schools are elated with state championships, but such trophies are not as meaningful as overall titles.

Class 1A teams like Loogootee no longer can experience the elation of trips to the Final Four and the thrill of meeting a 4A Marion for the state title. Underdogs made tournaments exciting, upsets added to the drama. Davids no longer can face Goliaths.

Multi-class basketball has been a factor in the move of adults — as well as students — to other venues, other attractions. Basketball is no longer the only game in town.

Much of the decline in interest, though, is the change in teenage culture. Take BNL. A lot of students were in the cheer section when I played. The pep band was there; it was part of the heritage, part of the event. It no longer is there for every game. I am told it needs to be at as many girls' games as boys' and not all the members want to perform that often.

Teens have more options for the use of their time. Boys basketball competes with girls' games for crowds. Athletes who once only had basketball to play can now compete for spots on teams that range from gymnastics to swimming to soccer. Fans are attracted to video games, DVDs, home entertainment options. Other teens prefer to work for spending money rather than play or attend games.

All those things have diminished interest in high school basketball. So have the politics of class basketball and the IHSAA's alignment of tournaments. It takes teams and fans

90 minutes in some cases to reach sectional sites, longer for some to drive to regional venues. It is impossible for fans who work until 5 p.m. to drive to 6 p.m. games on Tuesday nights.

Sectionals once were one-county or inter-county events. Now the games are between teams in other geographical areas, their players unfamiliar to fans.

It is more difficult for fans — even some athletes — to get inspired about a high school game or a state championship under the class system. Except for fans and players it is soon forgotten. It was a thrill for me to watch Scott Skiles lead his Plymouth team to the 1982 state title over big-city Gary Roosevelt. Had that been after class basketball started it would not have been possible because Plymouth would have played for the 3A, not the 4A championship.

I haven't watched more than one state championship game since class basketball started, nor I can tell you who won a state championship in any class last year. I don't care. It doesn't mean anything except to the fans and players who were involved.

Class basketball is like telling your child he is a winner because he is the top student in the bottom fourth of his class.

That declining interest among players and fans has led to a decline in the quality of play. So has Amateur Athletic Union competition. With the proliferation of AAU teams the talent is so diluted kids think they are better than they really are. Anyone it seems can play AAU basketball. No matter how good or how bad they are there is a team with a spot available.

When I played there were two or three outstanding AAU teams in each age division in the entire state. Only the best played. Now you have five or six AAU teams within cities the size of Bedford and some kids who can't make their high school teams in the winter are on summer teams.

Michael Jordan, you say, was once cut from a high school team, which is right. But for the most part, the growing number of AAU teams has reduced the level and given mediocre players a false hope of stardom. At one time, AAU basketball meant something and it was special. Teams played against the best players in the state and nation and if you won you had a trophy to treasure. Now, winning an AAU tournament doesn't mean as much because the level of competition is not as good.

Success doesn't mean as much because the opposition is not as good as it should be.

I do not expect any player to do what I did. The friends I played with did not put as much time into the game as I did, but they did spend a lot of hours at the game. They were better players because of it.

As elementary school students at Heltonville, three or four of us pre-teens were always playing, be it basketball, football or baseball. It is then when the small things about games are learned, when competition in whetted, when a player needs to start if he is to be good.

I no longer see that. Kids seldom play unless it is required, be that at an open gym, at practice or a game. They no longer go out and work on fundamentals to become better or even do it for fun. Rather than play in 90-degree heat, it is easier to sit at home and play Game Boy, Game Cube, Nintendo or whatever is the fad of the month.

Parents, usually by necessity in today's culture, live life in the fast lane. Many do not have the time that is needed to play with their youngsters, support their interests and give them encouragement.

Some parents who do want their children to play are into the blame game. Instead of being supportive, they blame the coach or the team because their sons or daughters have not played well. If that happens at games, it is certain to recur at home. That detracts from the child's desire to be good and he or she begins to think it is okay to condemn others for his faults.

I never made excuses for myself and my parents did not make excuses for me. If I did not play well, it was because it was something I did or did not do. It was not what the coach or a teammate had done or not done.

We will never see our children develop to their full potential if we continue to blame others. Both parents and their sons and daughters need to look into the mirror to see the source of the faults they place on others. The reflections they see will likely be themselves.

The result of all these things is that fewer great players are being developed in Indiana. And it leads up to what has happened at Indiana University where fewer and fewer players are being recruited from within the state.

Will it change? Perhaps, but it will be difficult unless high school basketball becomes more popular with fans and more Hoosier teens become more dedicated to the sport.

It may be too far along. Society today may not allow it. You will find one or two kids here and there who are success stories, but I think the level of talent coming out of Indiana is not what it once was.

That has to do with all the things I mentioned. I was and still am opposed to multi-class basketball, although I can understand it was done to give smaller schools a chance to win state championships. But I do not understand it at all from a competitive standpoint.

Life is not fair. Business is not fair. Just because a team is from a small school does not mean players cannot work to become the best they can be and compete against the largest schools. It penalizes kids from smaller schools, who will never know the extent of their greatness or what it is like to reach goals that are assumed beyond their abilities.

I think society today too often does not encourage players and schools to work to achieve goals beyond expectations. Too many players are not being encouraged to overcome adversity and obstacles and, as a result, they want things given to them. They want things changed to fit their needs and that is what happened. That happened when a small 1-A or 2-A school no longer could compete with a bigger 3-A or 4-A school.

That is a wrong message. Once these kids get out and go to college, or go to work in the real world, it no longer matters. A candidate for a job from a small school will need to compete with one from a larger school, not just with those from other Class 1A schools.

Success will be determined by how hard a person works and what he or she can accomplish. No one from a small school will be given special consideration over a worker from a larger school. Everyone has to compete on a level playing field.

Other Factors

As I noted in the section on my camps, fundamentals no longer seem to be important. They have been for the most part, cast aside.

Young players admire NBA players like Reggie Miller, Kobe Bryant, Alan Iverson, Vince Carter, Michael Jordan for their athletic ability, their shooting touches, their ball handling and dramatic passes. What they don't realize is that each is successful because he is fundamentally sound and has spent a lot of time in gyms perfecting those skills. Few athletes are born great. Those who become so are those who choose to work hard.

Teen-agers see those stars run the floor, be athletic, make behind the back passes, hit three point shots, dunk and score. They do not realize how much basketball intelligence those players have.

Even today Reggie Miller spends an amazing amount of time in the gym each day at work on his game. He was not born a great shooter and he doesn't continue to be as good as he is without continuing to shoot one shot after another each day.

Those players practice with their team, sure, but they put in a lot of time before and after practice working on the things that make them better.

Kids have got to get back to the basics of basketball or the quality will continue to decline, especially here in Indiana where we once played basketball the way it should be played.

From a personal viewpoint, it takes the cooperation of parents for players to be good. My parents, as I have said, spent countless days, driving me all over the country so I could play against the best players and the best competition. They missed time off work and overlooked their own interests for my benefit. Dad worked with me in the driveway or at the gym when he could have relaxed in front of the television.

Sure I had an advantage over youngsters who did not have parents to help them. Larry Bird didn't have that help, but he had a great work ethic plus a determination, dedication and a desire to just outwork the competition. That desire is rare today. His achievements can serve as a reminder that others can be a Larry Bird from French Lick, Indiana, without having great natural talent or special advantages.

Bird understood the game, knew a pass to a teammate for a basket counted as much as one he made himself. He was fundamentally sound. Too many young players do not have those fundamentals or that work ethic. They think the game is scoring points and looking good instead of playing as a team and winning games. It is disappointing to me because that is not the way I was taught to play.

Larry Bird was one player I tried to emulate. Like Bird, I realized I might not have the natural ability of other players, but I had the desire to go out and work to make myself better than they were. If I wasn't as good as some player or if I didn't shoot as well as someone else, it was up to me to work harder to improve, not blame the coach for not giving me more playing time.

I also learned not to blame my teammates when we lost. I was told instead to help them become better. In doing so I made myself better. The result was we became better as a team.

It is different today. It is easier for parents to point fingers at someone else rather than at themselves or their own sons or daughters. It is easier than admitting the problem lies within themselves.

As a parent, I realize now how hard it is to teach discipline to youngsters and to spent the time it takes to help them achieve what they try to do. It is a lot easier to make excuses that you do not have the time.

I get disgusted at times sitting as a fan at football, baseball or basketball games and listening to parents in the stands complaining about the coach. They moan because he isn't doing this or won't try that instead. They should be noting what their child is doing wrong and plan to take the time to help him or her to be better.

Coaches receive too much blame — and maybe at times — too much credit. Some coaches, of course, are better than others, but most times it is the individual who is playing — not the coach — who is responsible for his inability.

Criticism seems to be growing and much of that in my opinion is a result of school consolidation in the 1960 and 1970s. At one time there were 12 high schools in Lawrence County which meant 100 to 200 players were on varsity and reserve teams.

Those players (mostly men because few schools then had girls' teams) learned something about the game and knew a foul when they saw it, realized the discipline and drive that was needed to play. When they watched their sons and daughters play later, those men knew something about the game and realized coaches needed good players to be successful.

Since consolidation, seldom more than 25 players are on varsity and reserve teams at either Bedford North Lawrence or Mitchell, the two remaining schools.

Instead of hundreds of parents who had played the game, the number had been reduced by 80 percent or more. The critics had outnumbered those who at least knew something about the game. The same is true for baseball.

In my class we had 70 or 80 parents who had played high school basketball. That number declines each year and now ten years later there are very few parents who played on high school teams.

Some parents who have not played may not know a lot about the game. They may give their sons and daughters some wrong advice about how basketball is played.

Often it is parents who have not played who also are the most critical of coaches and other players. They pick up the lingo by watching games on TV and become instant experts. I seldom hear parents who know the game — or have been involved in their children's lives — criticize coaches or other players. They detect, no matter how good their own sons and daughters are, weaknesses that can be improved. They do not shift the blame onto the coach or other players.

Each coach has his own idea of how he wants his team to play. One idea is not necessarily better than another. Sure! Coaches can make mistakes, so can referees, but it is players who decide most games.

Early Departures

Sure, I hate to see players opt to go directly from high school to the National Basketball Association draft. The fault lies not with the teen-age players, but with NBA itself.

LeBron James for example will become a millionaire the day he leaves high school. What teen wouldn't take that?

It is easy for someone who has a job, a home, a car, economic security and all the benefits of a good life to criticize an 18-year-old for skipping college — or to leave early — to become a professional player. They have a good life and some of these young and talented players have nothing and have backgrounds that indicate life otherwise would be dismal.

No 18-year-old in those circumstances would pass up that opportunity. Nor would college coaches, who may criticize James for doing so.

I do agree the NBA needs to take action, perhaps, similar to what the National Football League has done to block a direct route from high school to the NFL.

It has to be difficult for a majority of kids coming directly into the NBA from high school. The changes are emotional, the lifestyle different, the transition too sudden, much more so than the switch from high school to college which itself is trying. It is the first time most kids are away from parental control and independent for the first time. The freshman year is difficult.

College provides an opportunity for players to adjust to a higher level of play, to develop maturity and to learn to cope with new situations. A direct route to a professional team, where associates are older, more worldly is an entirely different environment.

Few teens are ready, either physically or mentally, for that abrupt change. The NBA has been fortunate with players like Kevin Garnett, Kobe Bryant, Jermaine O'Neal and others who have done that. There have been, so far, no major problems with them. There are certain 18-year-olds who have shown they can cope under those circumstances, but most likely cannot.

To be fair to the NBA, it does try to spend time with the high school draftees and help them make the adjustment. Most older players are good role models, but some are not.

When a teen, with some guidance, can become a million-aire overnight and financially secure for life, who can blame him?

Pay for Players?

It may surprise some people for me to say this, but I think, to a degree, that college players should be paid. It would be difficult to control, even more so than it is now when some college players — not in Indiana — are or have been paid.

I don't know how many, probably not a lot. It would be worse if it was legal to do so. A monetary limit would have to be set and whatever that limit is it would have to be monitored. That would be difficult. It would result in more scandals than what we have today, even with the restrictions in place.

Nevertheless, I do think college athletes should be paid. People say they do get paid in the form of a free education. Make no mistake, I am grateful for that.

But the amount of money I.U. made off Calbert Cheaney, me or anyone who played with us, far exceeds the amount our education cost. Even years after we graduate I.U. makes money off us — or from our likenesses if you will. Right now it is selling three separate *Sports Illustrated* covers which had pictures of Kent Benson, Isiah Thomas and me on the front. The covers come with small plaques.

Tom Coverdale for example is not getting a dime from the sales of jerseys with his number. Neither does any other player. And consider all the money the university receives from its television contracts, its NCAA revenues and other benefits it receives indirectly from the efforts of athletes.

I do think players should be paid, be they on the basketball or football teams, which are the primary sources of athletic income. This, of course, would be met with criticism from women and men on other teams, most of which are non-revenue producers.

But, to repeat, it would be a very difficult policy to implement, not only because it would be hard to monitor. Smaller Division I school likely would not be able to afford the cost.

It has been discussed by the NCAA, but I doubt if an agreement can be reached as to how to work it out. As I say it would be difficult to administer and subject to abuse and it might make for messier situations than we have seen in the past.

Speaking for one sport only, I think players on the Indiana University basketball team should be paid.

But I want to emphasize, any participant in any sport, including basketball and football, should be a student athlete, attend class, receive only the grade he or she earns, and graduate.

PERSONAL FAVORITES

Indiana Fans

To be a player at Indiana University is special. Few basketball programs mean as much to their fans as does the one at I. U.

Sure, UCLA, Duke and North Carolina have built traditions of excellence. They have great programs and great fans, but not to the depth or feverish degree as at Indiana.

In terms of what basketball means to entire states, I don't think any other program can compare to those at Indiana or Kentucky. The fervor surrounding other programs is not as passionate or widespread. Both Indiana and Kentucky carry the names of their states on their uniforms. The players are ambassadors for their states and what they do reflects on all the people who live in them.

Purdue fans often complain the Boilermakers do not get the same attention as Hoosier teams. That, I imagine, is because of the name Indiana is a part of that; it is their address, the term they used to address who they are even though Purdue also is a state school. That too is why Kentucky overshadows Louisville.

Indiana fans consider themselves extensions of the team, the players their representatives. They live their lives vicariously through the team and live and die with each

Damon goes for a basket in I.U.-Purdue game

victory or defeat. Fans care for the players, their welfare
and their futures, not just while they are playing for Indiana but forever. It doesn't matter if a player is the best or
worst on the team. He still is admired and liked by the fans,
who often seem to know more about the players than they
know about themselves.

Fans can recall incidents from games decades ago and
recall how many points Jimmy Rayl scored against Minnesota in the early 1960s. Even today, 10 years later, fans mention where they were and what they were doing when we
played certain games a decade ago.

I think that impact you have on the lives of people is the
most important thing about Indiana basketball. Fans not
only can recall incidents from a particular game, they can
vividly remember a season, a career, a certain shot and incidents even players have forgotten.

Hoosiers, be they in the stands or dressed in red in front
of a TV to savor each victory, despair in defeat, suffer long
summers without the game and are reborn with new vigor
when practice starts in the fall.

All that means a lot to anyone who has ever worn an
I.U. uniform. It is why former players can be seen at every
game. They are no longer on the roster but they are part of
the lore that is Indiana basketball. That makes being — or
having been — a part of a team special.

The reception players get from fans 10, 20, 30 years
later is phenomenal. Once a Hoosier, you are forever after a
Hoosier. Fans do not cheer you and forget you. It is a positive few other teams can match.

Favorite Team

As an Indiana player, the 1992-93 team was my favorite. We won the Big Ten with a 17-1 record and were, no doubt, the league's best team.

Others may argue the 1991-1992 team was better because it reached the Final Four. Ken Bikoff, an I.U. graduate who has an Internet site, notes that team had talent and would have gone into the championship game had not referees made some bad calls. He recalls, "You had Damon Bailey, Calbert Cheaney, Eric Anderson and Todd Leary, all guys who were willing to play their roles to win a title. They were fun to watch."

I don't know if the officials cost us the game or not. I just think we had a better team the following season.

We had lost Anderson and Jamal Meeks from that Final Four team. I was back as were Cheaney, Leary, Alan Henderson, Greg Graham, Matt Nover, Bryan Evans and Chris Reynolds. Pat Graham returned from a red shirt year because of an injury. The team had depth, talent and experience.

We entered the tournament with not only the conference title but had won 28 games. Fans were even more excited than usual when the NCAA tournament began.

We reached the Final Eight even though Henderson's play was restricted by a heavy brace because of an injury to his right knee late in the season. His lack of playing time was a factor in our 83-77 loss to Kansas.

Had that not happened I am certain we would have won the sixth national championship for Indiana. Kansas had a great team, but I think with a healthy Henderson we would have won that game and gone on to the championship.

It, however, was a season to remember, one we finished with a 31-4 record. That was an experience of which we were proud at the time and can reflect back on with satisfaction today.

* * *

I also enjoyed my senior year. I got along better with coach Knight then than any other year. Instead of the first three years when, according to him, I never "played hard," I began to play harder than anyone who had ever played. Or so he said. I did not think I played any harder than I had before. He may have said that thinking we might not be a very good team if he rode me too hard. But who knows?

Right or wrong I considered that 1993-1994 squad my team. I was a senior and Henderson and Evans were still underclassmen, so I was looked on as the leader by the coaches and players. Cheaney, a senior, had been the leader the previous season and I understood that. Each player has a role on the team and the roles change each season.

We had a good, but not great, team my senior year considering all the injuries. Evans dislocated his shoulder at times. I pulled an abdominal muscle during the Big Ten season which limited my practice time and hurt my conditioning. In games, the muscle was often reinjured, making healing difficult. It would remain sore throughout the season.

We reached the regional round of the NCAA tournament, losing to Boston College, 77-68.

I didn't hear many complaints from the coach that season. That was good, for as I have said, he would not summon me unless it was for criticism.

[Editor's Note: Damon Bailey averaged 19.6 points a game his senior year, including two outstanding games. He scored 29 points in a 96-84 upset of No. 1 Kentucky, leading coach Knight to say, "That's the best I've seen Bailey play," then, as usual added a note of sarcasm, saying, "This is how he was supposed to be able to play."

[A few weeks later, Bailey scored 36 points when I.U. lost an overtime thriller to highly-ranked Kansas, 86-83. Kansas coach Roy Williams told Bailey after the game, "That was one of the most sensational performances I have ever seen. You just kept putting your head down, driving to the hoop, getting fouled and hitting the free throws."]

Favorite Players

I have been a teammate with a lot of great players and many class individuals. Basketball, as I've said before is a team sport. The whole is more important than the individual.

To choose a few of my favorite teammates from the hundreds I have had at the AAU, junior high, high school, college and professional level is difficult. The few I have selected should not detract from my appreciation of dozens of others.

Among those favorite players are each of my teammates at Bedford North Lawrence. Despite all my attention, all the mentions in newspapers, magazines, radio broadcasts and television reports, there was no jealousy among them. That may have been because most of us had been friends for years. We had grown up together. They knew I had been the most valuable player on three national championship AAU teams from the time I was 11 years old, so they were accustomed to the attention I received. It was just part of their lives and I do not think they were bothered by it. I scored most of the points but each contributed in his own way, which allowed our 1990 team win the state championship.

I really enjoyed playing with Calbert Cheaney at I.U. even though I might have had a more impressive career — in term of scoring — had he not been there my first three years.

His presence enabled me and others to be on teams that won a lot of games, played in three NCAA tournaments and reached the Final Four one time.

If that hurt me from a standpoint of statistics so be it. Had that bothered me he would not have been a good player to be with on a team. I would surely have scored more points, but we would not have won as many games without him.

That aside, Cheaney is a super person who worked extremely hard in practice and in games. It was good to see him have a good season in 2002-2003 with the Utah Jazz in the NBA.

I really enjoyed playing with Calbert and I am grateful for the experience. And I am especially pleased to have had the assist on the basket Cheaney scored in 1993 to become Indiana's all-time leading scorer.

With the Pacers, at the professional level Byron Scott and Sam Mitchell were great people to be around. I learned a lot about the professional game from them. They were true professionals who treated basketball with respect. It was not, for them, a game where you awoke at 8 a.m., moseyed around for a while, loafed much of the day then played at night. They lifted weights, worked out each day and stayed in shape between seasons. And they knew how the game should be played. I hope they continue to get opportunities to coach in the NBA. I appreciated most of my teammates from each level I played. Almost all of them were willing to make sacrifices for the good of whatever team they were on.

Favorite Arenas

Purdue, believe it or not, was one of my favorite places to play. Mackey Arena is a great venue and the added drama of the IU-Purdue rivalry adds to the atmosphere.

To compete there in that hostile environment, to hear the boos, the chants, the venom from rabid enemy fans increases your desire to win. You remain an enemy even after you graduate. I remember being there with the Pacers for an exhibition game. I was booed loudly and long when my name was announced. I liked that. I was glad Purdue hated me for the teams I was on had a 6-2 game edge over my four years at I.U.

I was happy to hear the jeers. Had they cheered it would have likely meant Purdue had won more times than we did. It was definitely a fun place to play.

So was Penn State, which opened a new fieldhouse after I graduated from Indiana. We played in the old arena, which seated 8,000 fans but looked like a high school gym. Students were seated right off the floor, so close they could push you in the back and often did. They were vocal, which was good, because, as I noted, the louder the opposition fans are the harder you want to play.

To me the best places to play are those where the rivalry is strong or where you've had good games in the past. As was noted in the movie "Hoosiers," the floors are all the same length and the goals the same height. That is true, but no two arenas are the same. The surroundings are different and so are the crowds.

Rudest Fans

Michigan was a tough place to play, not only because of the great players who were there as part of its great Fab 5 teams but because of the students. They began their harassment as soon as we got off the bus, pelting us with snowballs on each visit because we always seemed to arrive right after another snowstorm.

The bus parked 20 feet away from a tunnel into the arena, which meant the students could launch their missiles along the way. In order to compete in basketball, we had to play dodgeball first and then walk through the same barrage en route to the bus when the game was over.

Inside the arena the fans were rabid and vicious and never stopped hurling insults.

I'll never forget an incident my freshman year. I was injured and sat beside Chris Lawson, who was in a "red-shirt" season. We kept hearing a feminine voice shout obscenities behind us that carried out onto the playing floor. We tried at time-outs to spot the woman in the crowd but failed to pick her out until late in the game. She was at least 70 years old and just three rows behind us.

As we looked in amazement in her direction she began an obscene tirade, choosing Lawson for some reason as her target. "F . . . you, you big redhead."

Knowing we had been trying to locate her, she shouted, "It's me!" and continued her taunts, having forgotten any Sunday school lessons she had been taught. The more we laughed the more vulgar she became.

Chris and I could enjoy her tirade. But you can't imagine how hard it is to concentrate on the floor during those kinds of constant distractions.

Every game there, players would come into the dressing room at the half asking "Did you hear all that profanity and vulgarity?" It was always that way at Michigan.

Those are the types of experiences a player appreciates. It means the games are important to the students and to fans as well as entire cities and states.

I regret that we never had a chance to play at Duke, because that would have been a fun environment. Of course, if we had played and lost by 40 points, it would not have been enjoyable. Had we played and won or played well and lost, it would have been a memorable experience.

But those things make winning in rancorous arenas all the more pleasurable. It was always good to go into a hostile arena. It made us want to win even more than usual and whetted our competitive edge.

We lost the last game of the 1991-92 season at Purdue, a team we had drilled 105-65 a few weeks earlier. The unranked Boilermakers defeated us (we were ranked No. 4 at the time) 61-59, spoiling our chance for a tie with Ohio State for the conference title.

It was senior night, and seniors Woody Austin and Craig Riley responded with a combined 35 points in a game Purdue still ranks among its most exciting victories.

Riley summed up the rivalry that exists between the two schools: "To ruin their championship means everything. You cannot top it. This just makes my whole career."

Austin agreed. "It is the highlight of my career. We beat them in the final game . . . busted their hope for a Big Ten title and a No. 1 seed in the NCAA tournament."

Victories over the other mean that much to both Indiana and Purdue players. Rivalries like that are great, especially when you win. Nothing is sweeter than a victory over your worst enemy. Nothing is sweeter than flashing a victory smile at fans as they throw snowballs at you as you walk to the bus.

Loses to Purdue hurt coach Knight as much as they did the players. After we lost to the Boilermakers in 1992, coach canceled the awards banquet, which probably upset the fans, who had planned to attend, more than it did the players.

An autograph session a few weeks later gave fans an opportunity to meet the players, take our pictures and exchange a few words with us. It allowed each of us to learn how much we meant to the fans. The evening was more enjoyable than the banquet would have been.

IN RETROSPECT

It was a great honor to be selected to Indiana University's all-century basketball team, especially because it was an honor I could share with Isiah Thomas and Steve Alford, whom I grew up watching on television.

I did not play for honors. Like most players, I played to win. It is nice, however, to know that what you did deserved that kind of recognition.

Awards like that allow me to look back on my career with pride. I have read articles that question what I accomplished as a college player and I have heard coach Knight's comment about failure to meet expectations. It is a tribute to be grouped with the greatest players in I.U. history. To have that honor and the statistics I had that contributed to 108 Indiana victories, makes it even more special.

One comment coach Knight made has stuck with me and I've come to realize he had a point. He said the reason we play is not for ourselves, or the fans, or businessmen or even the university, nor to be lauded on magazine cover, on TV, or in newspapers. We play, not only for the team, he said, but for those who have illnesses and misfortunes that do not allow them to have the opportunities we have.

Indiana players make a difference in the lives of other Hoosiers. I was happy to do that. For me, one of those persons was Megan Easterday. I met her through a letter she wrote to the Indiana Pacers at a time she suffered with terminal cancer. We corresponded for a time before I joined the Fury and had a chance to visit her in a Fort Wayne hospital. She was, by coincidence, one of the patients helped by a charity in which Jay Leonard, one of the Fury owners, was involved. It is good to know players can bring joy to people in unfortunate circumstances who do not have the pleasures life has given athletes.

As I said, a player does not compete for recognition, but once you no longer play such claims are treasures to value. It reminds you that your career was valued even when others may have had doubts.

My personality may have, at times, hurt me as an individual and detracted from my statistics. I put more of an emphasis on winning and I was content if we won. A victory meant more to me than any individual results posted in the scorebook.

I averaged just under 20 points a game my senior year. I think I could have done that each of the four years I was at I.U. Would we have won as many games or done as well in the Big Ten or the NCAA tournament had I done that? Probably not. I just tried to help the team win games and was content with whatever my points were if I had shared the ball and done what I could to win.

That emphasis hurt me in the CBA. Scouts from the NBA put a big emphasis on statistics. I would rather win than average 20 points a game. The last year I was in that league I often scored 20 points a game on a team with good shooters. In contrast there were games when no one on our team would score 20 because we shared the points. It didn't matter to me. I knew I might have to score 30 in a game later if other players were injured.

Looking back, that emphasis on the team probably was not the best thing for me as an individual. It was, however, the best thing for the team.

Are players today willing to make that sacrifice? Very few — a select few — are in my opinion, probably fewer than in the past. The game is so individually oriented today, often at the expense of victories. I thought if the team I was on won, I would get individual recognition when it was deserved. I saw no point in piling up statistics to get attention in a loss.

It is a team — not an individual — sport, something some players of today forget.

Most of our I.U. teams were made up of players who put winning ahead of personal accomplishments. Oh, there may have been a few who were interested in personal output, but winning was the major goal.

With the Fury some players sought to build big numbers in an effort to gain NBA attention. That changed when Keith Smart became coach. He brought in team players and that helped us build a good team.

That is why they keep score for each team, instead of having one scorebook for each player. Individuals may have a good game one night, a bad game the next. Good teams, not me-first players, win games and championships. Teams with players who put themselves first struggle.

Television, in my opinion, is partly to blame for much of the emphasis on self rather than team. Sit and watch Sports Center and you see that what stands out are great individual plays or great dunks. It is not who won. The Lakers might have just won their ninth straight game, but the reports center on Kobe Bryant's 50 points. Individuals get more attention than teams.

It is the entire mentality of the media — of society — in general. That accent is the direct opposite of what basketball should be. It is a result of a me-first mentality.

Referees

I never liked any referees. No, I'm just kidding. They are a necessary part of the game.

I never said much to them on any team I played. Coach Bush at BNL did not want us to complain to referees and at I.U. coach Knight did enough griping that any lament by his players would be adding raindrops to a downpour.

There were some good referees at the high school level but I never knew their names. We seldom had the same officials more than one or two times each season so we did not really get to know them and there was very little conversation between us.

In college and professional you see the same referees a lot, regardless of whether you like them or not. Steve Welmer of Columbus was one of the better ones, or so I thought. Ted Hillary was another one as was Ed Hightower.

Hillary, who lives in Michigan, came to some of our Fury games when we played at Grand Rapids and I enjoyed talking to him then.

The best referees are the ones you don't notice. If they are good, you hardly know they are there. They call the games, control the action but leave the attention to the players. I never liked Ted Valentine for that reason. He puts on a show, in my opinion, and referees are not there for that reason. Fans do not pay to see referees. They spend money to see teams.

I never complained much. Like players, referees all make mistakes and some will admit it when they do. I might not have agreed with the calls, but I just handed them the ball and forgot about it. I think you gain respect from officials when you do not try to taunt or make them look bad.

They are under stress from coaches and fans. They do not need the added distraction of whining players. And it is become more difficult each year to referee. Players become more athletic, the pace of game gets faster, fans become more hostile and players get more vocal.

Sideline Experts

DICK VITALE. I enjoy listening to him. He is an entertainer. Dickie V is someone people either love, or hate, to listen to. He can be overbearing. His repetition of his favorite clichés may be tiresome, but he works at it. He does what he can do to be knowledgeable about the game. He gives insight.

I've heard his speeches and they are interesting shows. He rants, raves, moves around and is soaked with sweat when he finishes. He is full of energy. You have to admire someone who works at his job as hard as Vitale does.

BILLY PACKER: I am not a big Billy Packer fan. He has his favorite teams and all other teams are secondary. If you are not an ACC team, to him, you are not very good, or so he seems to observers.

Packer has never seemed to be a Big Ten fan and I am sure he must have been disappointed in 2002 when I.U. beat Duke before losing the final game of the NCAA tournament.

That did not, however, stop him from saying before the 2003 tournament that any run by a Big Ten team would be "short and sweet." It turned out two Big Ten teams reached the Final 16.

ISIAH THOMAS: I do not know Isiah so I do not have a personal opinion. He looks like a great guy on TV, which is about all I can say.

BILL WALTON: He is full of confidence and, based on his career in basketball, he has a right to his opinions. He goes overboard at times but he does offer a lot of insight to the game from a player's standpoint.

DIGGER PHELPS: I respect him and I enjoy listening to his comments. He made a few overtures to recruit me and I know from playing against his Notre Dame teams that he is very knowledgeable about the game. He has a great personality and I rate him among the top television analysts in basketball.

QUINN BUCKNER: He is not as polished as some of the critics, but he can break down a game as well as anyone.

I put more stock in what former players say than in critics like Packer, Vitale and Jim Nantz. They are entertainers. If they played or coached it was years ago and the game has changed in the meantime. They get excited about a behind the back pass or a slam dunk. We can observe that for ourselves. We don't need them to tell us what we have seen.

Color commentators like Bob Leonard on the Pacers radio network or Quinn Buckner who does some Pacers television games can tell us about facets of the game we might not see or hear from the play-by-play announcers.

THE FUTURE

Politics

I am often asked if I would be interested in running for a political or some other elective office. I have, likely because of my name recognition, been approached by both Democrats and Republicans about a possible candidacy.

But at this time, I'm just not ready to be involved. I would never say never, but never may be far into the future. Like professional basketball, it would take time from my family and my business and I'm not willing to be distracted from either.

A majority of people, it seems to me, run for office, be it the county council, the school board or even for president for the wrong purposes. Consider the three reasons candidates seek office:

* They sincerely want to make a difference, to help their constituents and to use their talent to do the right thing. Those are good and noble reasons.

* For recognition. They want to be somebody in the eyes of others, to be seen as important, to seek fame. Those obviously are not good reasons.

* Because they have a personal agenda or an axe to grind. They feel offended by someone, their sons or daughters were cut from an athletic team or suspended from

school, or they feel they've been snubbed by someone in office.

That happens a lot at the local level. A candidate for school board may have an agenda to fire the superintendent, the principal, an athletic director or a coach rather than to improve education. Those, of course, are the wrong reasons. I do think there are things I would like to accomplish or to help improve. But I'm "old school" with traditional values. The opinions I have might not be the same as those of a majority of voters. The world keeps changing, as it always has, and what I might believe should be done might not be accepted by society today.

What office might I consider later? I don't know. I'm not aware of what all is involved with a political office or the responsibilities it entails. I do not know the entire role of a state legislator or all the responsibilities of the Indiana House or Indiana Senate. I would certainly learn everything the job required before I would seek any office no matter how minor or how significant.

What is government's role? I am not someone who looks to the government to help me. I do not, however, want it to harm me. I do not think whoever is in office should face continual criticism. We need to trust the people we elect to represent us. We should trust the president and let him do his job. When he faces re-election he can be voted out of office if a majority of people disagree with what he does. Meantime, rely on him to make the decisions he was elected to make.

He knows more than the "expert analysts," talking heads and entertainment personalities who fill television screens with opinions that are no more valid than yours or mine. He does not need demonstrators to cloud the issues.

Business is built on trust. Government should be also.

Sports And Our Children

I do want our three children to be involved in sports. Team athletics are good for young people and the benefits exceed the negatives.

Sports teach teamwork and competitiveness, they allow young people to interact with kids their age and teach teamwork needed to accomplish goals, to have coaches and to take orders or directions from other people than just their moms and dads.

I encourage any kid to get involved in activities like that. Our girls are involved in gymnastics, cheerleading and T-ball and I am sure Brayton will be into competitive sports when he is older.

My kids in particular may face some negatives because they are Damon Bailey's kids. If Brayton plays basketball he may face criticism that he isn't as good as I was. I am sure I will expect him as well as the girls to be very good at what they choose.

I may not choose to coach their teams, but I will work with them to be better. I work with my girls now, not on cheerleading because that is Stacey's forte, not mine, but with T-ball. I believe if you are going to play — or have a job — that you need to work to be as good as you can be. That is one thing I will stress. If they do something they will be expected to do it right, to work at it and be the best their abilities will allow.

I may not expect them to work as hard as I did, or to be the best. I will tell them that to get anywhere in life it takes work, that little is given. It doesn't mean they have to be great   T-Ball   players,   great   cheerleaders   or   Olympic gymnasts or star basketball players. It does mean to survive; they need to work and be competitive.

I expect, as I said, for my kids to face criticism. If they reach a point they don't want to hear it or no longer want to be involved, I will understand.

I won't force Brayton to play basketball. If he grows up and decides baseball or football or something else is his sport, that will be fine. If that is the case and he plays football he will have to work at it, same for baseball or whatever.

Coaching

I am asked almost daily if I would ever want to coach. It is a question I consider with mixed emotions and cannot honestly answer at this stage in my life.

I have grown to miss the game, the thrills of the competition and the joy of victories. That absence has left a void within me. So I never say never when the question arises.

A decision to coach would not be made lightly because I would be dedicated to it and give it my total commitment. I would coach the way I think it should be done and spend the time and effort it takes to make my teams the best their talents and my direction allowed.

I do know it would take hours and days of preparation. I am not prepared at this point to yield those hours away from my family or my business.

Nothing would please me more than to help young players improve their games, watch them progress, set goals and see them strive to meet those expectations.

Teams cannot just show up for games and expect to win. Most games are won before they start. They are won through preparation and practice, both of which take time.

Another reason why I might never coach is the attitude of a lot of players today. Too many might not want to do the work, accept the style of play I would demand or expend the effort I would require. I would expect them to do what it would take to be winners. Victory, after all, is the objective and why scores are kept.

As competitive as I am, it would drive me crazy if players did not have that same desire to be good and to become winners. As I have said, I do not think a lot of young players today have that desire to be competitive enough to become winners.

I would not only want to be competitive but I would want to win. I work hard and I would expect my players to do the same. Excuses would not be accepted. But to repeat myself, it is doubtful if many players would have that drive and I doubt if a coach could make those demands in today's sympathetic society.

Coach Bush at BNL hated to lose. Each of us on the team had the same drive. We hated to lose more than we liked to win. The fear of losing drove us. The fact we had not lost equaled the thrill of victory.

It would be extremely frustrating for me as a coach if the players did not have that same drive.

Too many players today see basketball as a diversion, a way to have fun, a chance to be recognized as individuals, not as a part of the team. A team needs individuals who view the team as more important than themselves.

A lot of players today think basketball starts in October. There is neither a start nor an end for young players, it is continuous if they are to be good. Parents might not agree with the demands I would place on their sons or want them to be as deeply involved.

This is not a criticism of parents and players. It is a reflection of a society that has allowed life's easiest roads to be the most traveled, bypassing any conflicts or interruptions along the way. Our lives for the most part have become too easy and far too many people expect rewards without efforts.

Despite all those drawbacks, I might eventually coach for it would be something I enjoy, an extension of what we are able to do now on a limited basis at my camps. Those camps, with my limited time now, are a good way to help young kids become good players.

SELF ASSESSMENT

Was I, as a player, a combination of natural ability and hard work? I had some athletic ability but I was not as good an athlete as the Bryants and Jordans. I wasn't nearly as tall or as quick. I did work hard each day on my game, but certainly not as hard as Larry Bird.

In retrospect, I am not disappointed in the effort I put forth. I worked hard to become the player I was. Could I have worked harder? Yes, I could have. Did I work absolutely as hard as I could? No.

The desire to work on my game waned later in my basketball career. I think there were three reasons why the time I put into basketball was not equal to what it was in high school:

* As a freshman, I was, as others have experienced, away from home and my parents for the first time. Parents are no longer there to make you go to practice, be it basketball or choir. They cannot make you do your homework or work out in the gym and they are not there to order you from bed and see that you attend classes.

* I had some injuries as an upperclassman at I.U. that did not allow me to practice as much as I should. I needed to be ready to play the next game and couldn't risk further injury in practice.

* I was married and a father by the time I was a professional player and I needed to — and wanted to — devote time to my family and to my business as well as to my basketball team. Those were my choices and I am happy I made them.

It was a time when my mind recalled the occasions when my parents told me there would be days in the future when I would wish I was back in high school. I scoffed at the thought then, sure that day would never come.

I know I had none of the responsibilities of adulthood, bills to pay, food and medicine to buy, a company to help run. All I had to do was make good grades, play basketball as well as I could and cut wood for the fire. Otherwise, as with most teen-agers, I had not a care in the world.

Life, I would learn, is not the same after high school.

That aside I would not want to return to that age. Life requires choices; family and work obligations take time. My family and my business are more important than basketball no matter how much I miss the game.

We all talk about giving 100 percent to what we do, but I do not know one person — successful or not — who works as a hard as he or she can. I work hard at business, I've been here since 6 a.m. and will be here to 5 p.m. It will be a long day. Could I stay here another hour and accomplish even more? Probably.

You need to be happy with the amount of time you put into what you choose to do. From that standpoint I can honestly say I am. I can look at myself and know I've worked very hard to accomplish what I've been able to accomplish. That is satisfaction in itself.

Sure, there have been objectives I did not get done. But I can be content with the effort I gave and with how things have turned out.

I seldom have a basketball in my hand now other than the barnstorming tours we make each spring. I do work out some for those games. I still lift weights and run for health reasons, but I don't work out on a regular schedule.

Otherwise, I don't really have that much interest. There really isn't anywhere to play except at the HYPER Building at I.U. or the Boys Club gym in Bedford. The way my dad and other men got together and played at Heltonville or at the Oolitic gym doesn't happen anymore. If I called some people and asked them to play somewhere they would do it, but it wouldn't be the same. I enjoyed basketball from a competitive standpoint. It gave me a challenge to overcome and a way to improve my ability. That is what I enjoyed. I did shoot a lot in non-competitive practice, but that was because I wanted to be better than the next person.

I am competitive be it at a game of ping pong, golf or video games. I hate to lose be it business or ping pong. I am going to try to win, no matter the competition. I play a lot of ping pong and golf with Josh Allen, who I knew when he was growing up at Heltonville and later as a player at Bedford North Lawrence. And he keeps reminding me that no one is more competitive than I am.

I don't know where that drive comes from. It is just a switch that comes on when it comes to winning. We may sit here and decide to play ping pong and something clicks. My body feels completely different and I am going to do my best to win. I don't know if it was something I was born with, it was instilled by my parents, my own determination, or a combination of all those things.

*   *   *

Editor's Note: Josh Allen, who worked part time as a college student at the Hawkins Bailey Warehouse, agrees. "Damon is indeed a competitive guy," he noted, then cites as an example.

"We played ping pong at a table there in the warehouse for a time before it became serious competition. Damon could beat me badly for a long time before we started wagering small amounts to give us a reason to win. He was better, even though I hate to admit it.

"Those bets never phased him until we agreed the losers of a doubles match would have their head shaved there at the warehouse. It must have been the fear of having that done that caused Damon to choke. For what may have been the first time in his life he was nervous under pressure.

"Naturally Damon was upset. He tried everything to avoid that shaved head, even had his wife Stacey and one of his daughters call us and plead for mercy. He even tried monetary rewards, but we didn't relent.

"He arrived at work the next morning wearing a hat. His head was shaved but he had denied me the honor of wielding the scissors. That ping pong victory was one of the most gratifying moments of my young life."

Allen admits that, except for that one ping pong game, Damon competes better under the pressure of competition. "I am a better golfer than he is and he admits that. But that competitive edge gives him an advantage. He won the last time we played with a 75 to my 76."

Allen, who has worked at the Damon Bailey Camps since graduating from BNL in 1999, calls the camps well run. "Damon and Dave Carrington make a good team and the addition of I.U. players as counselors have made the camps even better."

And he adds, "Damon is a good employer. He can be hard-nosed as all employers need to be at times and he and Randy Hawkins work well together. And don't think the Bailey name is on the business for Damon's fame. He has learned the business well, knows what he is talking about and is well acquainted with every product the firm sells."

Allen helped Damon coach a fourth grade AAU team in Bedford last summer. "It was obvious he can coach and the kids seem to love him. They had fun and so did we," Allen said.

IN TEN YEARS?

It seems fashionable these days to be asked where we expect to be ten years down the road. Circumstances change and we sometimes cannot dictate the future.

With no unforeseen deviations, I expect to be involved in business as I am now. I enjoy coming to work, dealing with our customers and our employees. Business is competitive and challenging and, as I have said, requires many of the attributes of basketball; cooperation, teamwork, imagination and ingenuity.

I learn something new about business every day even though I have been involved full time for almost four years and part-time since 1994. I've been fortunate to be surrounded by some very good people, who have been successful in business and who have helped me learn what needs to be done to be successful.

Randy and I do not always agree; neither do Jay Frye, a partner with Krispy Kreme donuts, and me. But we are able to reach a compromise if we cannot change each other's minds. Once we reach an agreement, we go on and forget those differences of opinion.

So ten years ahead, I expect to be even more involved in business, whether we grow the Hawkins Bailey Warehouse or branch out into additional endeavors.

I certainly want to be involved with my children's activities. Our daughters will be in their teens and I am certain they will be engaged in sports and other activities as they are now. Son Brayton will be approaching adolescence and I'm sure he will be just as busy.

Activities help them mature and I want to see them participate and be competitive in whatever endeavors they choose. And I want to share my time with them as my parents did with me.

*   *   *

I will forever be grateful for the support of my family, my coaches and the fans. I am now beyond the glory I received, but it will always be a part of me. No one could ask for better memories.

ALSO AVAILABLE

Damon - Living A Dream: Damon Bailey's first book that details his career through college. Price by mail $17.00 (includes postage and sales tax).

Send orders:

Backroads Press
P. O. Box 651
Mooresville IN 46158